Microsoft Certification Books from Sybex

Azure Certifications

MC Microsoft Certified Azure Data Fundamentals Study Guide: Exam DP-900 — ISBN 978-1-119-85583-5, April 2022

Edition with accompanying online labs — ISBN 978-1-394-15845-4, August 2022

Microsoft Azure Architect Technologies and Design Complete Study Guide: Exams AZ-303 and AZ-304 — ISBN 978-1-119-55953-5, December 2020

MCA Microsoft Certified Associate Azure Administrator Study Guide: Exam AZ-104 — ISBN 978-1-119-70515-4, April 2022

Edition with accompanying online labs — ISBN 978-1-394-15847-8, August 2022

Microsoft Certified Azure Fundamentals Study Guide: Exam AZ-900 — ISBN 978-1-119-77092-3, April 2021

MCA Microsoft Certified Associate Azure Network Engineer Study Guide: Exam AZ-700 — ISBN 978-1-119-87292-4, September 2022

MCA Microsoft Certified Associate Azure Security Engineer Study Guide: Exam AZ-500 — ISBN 978-1-119-87037-1, November 2022

Microsoft 365 Certifications

MCA Microsoft 365 Teams Administrator Study Guide: Exam MS-700 — ISBN 978-1-119-77334-4, September 2021

MCA Modern Desktop Administrator Complete Study Guide with 900 Practice Test Questions: Exam MD-100 and Exam MD-101, 2nd Edition — ISBN 978-1-119-98464-1, January 2023

MCE Microsoft Certified Expert Cybersecurity Architect Study Guide: Exam SC-100 — ISBN 978-1-394-18021-9, April 2023

MCA Windows Server Hybrid Administrator Complete Study Guide with 400 Practice Test Questions: Exam AZ-800 and Exam AZ-801 — ISBN 978-1-394-15541-5, May 2023

Microsoft Office 365 Certifications

MCA Microsoft Office Specialist (Office 365 and Office 2019) Complete Study Guide: Word Exam MO-100, Excel Exam MO-200, and PowerPoint Exam MO-300 — ISBN 978-1-119-71849-9, June 2021

MCA Microsoft Office Specialist (Office 365 and Office 2019) Study Guide: Word Associate Exam MO-100 — ISBN 978-1-119-71826-0, December 2020

MCA Microsoft Office Specialist (Office 365 and Office 2019) Study Guide: Excel Associate Exam MO-200 — ISBN 978-1-119-71824-6, March 2021

MCA Microsoft Office Specialist (Office 365 and Office 2019) Study Guide: PowerPoint Associate Exam MO-300 — ISBN 978-1-119-71846-8, May 2021

GitHub Copilot Certification

Study Guide

Tom Taulli

A Wiley Brand

Published by John Wiley & Sons, Inc., Hoboken, New Jersey.
Published simultaneously in Canada.

For general information on our other products and services, please contact our Customer Care Department within the United States at (800) 762-2974, outside the United States at (317) 572-3993. For product technical support, you can find answers to frequently asked questions or reach us via live chat at https://sybexsupport.wiley.com.

If you believe you've found a mistake in this book, please bring it to our attention by emailing our reader support team at wileysupport@wiley.com with the subject line "Possible Book Errata Submission."

Wiley also publishes its books in a variety of electronic formats. Some content that appears in print may not be available in electronic formats. For more information about Wiley products, visit our web site at www.wiley.com.

Library of Congress Cataloging-in-Publication Data Applied For:

Paperback ISBN: 9781394349982
ePDF ISBN: 9781394349999
ePub ISBN: 9781394350001

Cover Design: Wiley
Cover Image: © Jeremy Woodhouse/Getty Images

Contents at a Glance

Contents

Acknowledgments

In early December 2024, I submitted a proposal for this book in the Wiley portal—and I crossed my fingers. The next day, I got an email from Kenyon Brown, a senior acquisitions editor at the company. He said my timing was perfect, and he was interested in pursuing the book. In less than two weeks, I had a signed contract.

So yes, I want to thank Kenyon for his belief in the project and his speed. But I also want to thank Krysta Winsheimer, a project manager and senior editor. She made the writing and editing process very smooth. Whenever I had a question, I would get a prompt response. She would even respond during weekends.

All in all, working with Wiley has been a great experience.

About the Author

Tom Taulli is a self-taught developer. He learned programming when he was a freshman in high school, during the early 1980s. He joined a local user's group, where he met Bill Gates, Peter Norton, and Phillipe Kahn. This inspired him to sell his own software and publish articles in computer magazines.

In college, Tom started a company to help students prepare for certification exams. He raised capital for the firm, and he would go on to launch several other companies, such as Hypermart.net (the company was sold to InfoSpace).

Along the way, Tom kept writing. He authored several books about software development and AI, including *Artificial Intelligence Basics: A Non-Technical Introduction* and *AI-Assisted Programming: Better Planning, Coding, Testing, and Deployment.* He has also written articles for publications like BusinessWeek.com, Boomberg.com, and Inc.com.

As for leveraging AI for software development, he started this within a couple months of when GitHub Copilot was launched. He would go on to develop courses for this, such as for PluralSight and O'Reilly Media.

You can reach Tom at `https://www.linkedin.com/in/tomtaulli/`.

About the Technical Editor

Vaclav Jirovsky began his career in IT as a system administrator but quickly moved into software development. Over the years, he's taken on a variety of roles—including solution architect, UI designer, and product manager—which has given him a well-rounded perspective on the entire software development lifecycle. His diverse experience helps him understand both the technical and user-focused sides of building software.

Vaclav enjoys exploring new and emerging technologies. Lately, he's been exploring AI-powered tools like GitHub Copilot to boost productivity in software development.

You can reach Vaclav at `www.linkedin.com/in/vaclavjirovsky/`.

Introduction

One of the early use cases of modern generative AI was code generation. A couple years before the launch of ChatGPT in late 2022, OpenAI made Codex available as a private beta API. The system was fine-tuned on billions of lines of public repositories and could generate code for various languages. Codex proved to be extremely popular. The technology also became the basis of GitHub Copilot.

Since then, the underlying generative models have made giant leaps in progress. They can process enormous amounts of data, use advanced reasoning, and process information in real time.

Now, AI coding is becoming an essential part of a developer's toolbelt. Even people with little or no technical experience can create useful applications—something that has become known as *vibe coding*.

In the Stack Overflow's 2024 Developer Survey—which included more than 65,000 responses from developers—76 percent of the respondents said they were using or plan to use AI tools.[1] The survey also showed that 41.2 percent said they use GitHub Copilot.

In light of these trends, it should be no surprise that AI coding skills are becoming more important for landing a new job in software development or getting promoted. Employers want their teams to be more productive and to create higher quality code.

A great way to showcase your capabilities with AI coding is to get the GitHub Copilot certification. It covers key topics like responsible AI, how the system works and uses data, techniques for prompt engineering, developer use cases, and software testing.

Achieving the certification will help you stand out with employers. It can not only help get you a new job but also improve your compensation. There may also be more job security.

The goal of this book is to provide the resources you need to pass the exam. It is written to provide a step-by-step process to learning the key topics and concepts.

In fact, this book covers more than passing the exam. You also learn strategies and techniques to get the most out of your AI coding tasks.

What Is GitHub Copilot?

GitHub Copilot is a platform that allows you to use natural language for software development. For example, you can write a prompt like *Write a Python function that filters out all odd numbers from an array.* GitHub Copilot will process this using a sophisticated generative AI model and generate a response. It will not only include the generated code but also an explanation.

GitHub Copilot is more than creating code. You can also use it for debugging, refactoring, testing, and creating descriptions for pull requests. You can even use it to learn a language, framework, or library.

GitHub Copilot is a versatile tool, and it is undergoing much innovation. This book covers some of the latest features, like Edits, even though they are not currently on the exam (but are likely to be in the future).

GitHub Copilot Certification Exam

Besides the GitHub Copilot certification exam, there are four other certifications available:

- **GitHub Foundations:** This covers the fundamental topics of using GitHub and Git, such as with understanding repositories, commits, branching, and pull requests.

- **GitHub Actions:** This is focused on understanding the development workflows, automations, and continuous integration and continuous delivery/deployment (CI/CD) pipelines.

- **GitHub Advanced Security:** This exam tests your knowledge about GitHub security features like secret scanning, dependency management, code scanning, and analysis with CodeQL.

- **GitHub Administration:** This is about how to optimize and manage a GitHub environment.

GitHub does not require any perquisites for these exams. The company also does not provide the level of difficulty. But generally, GitHub Foundations is at a beginner level, whereas the others are more advanced.

Besides software developers, the GitHub Copilot exam can be a good fit for administrators and project managers, but you should have a basic understanding of software development.

The GitHub Copilot certification consists of 65 multiple-choice questions and there is a two-hour limit. The exam is available in English, Portuguese, Spanish, Korean, and Japanese. The fee is $99 in the United States.

When you pass the exam, you will receive a digital badge, which you can place on your social media channels. The certification is valid for three years.

You can take the exam online or in person at a local test center, which is proctored by PSI. To register for the exam, go to `https://examregistration.github.com/certification/COPILOT`.

You will need a valid government-issued ID that has your name, photo, and signature. Make sure that your first and last name on it matches what you enter in the registration form for the exam.

Becoming Certified for GitHub Copilot

The best approach to preparing for the GitHub Copilot exam is to read this book from start to finish. Each chapter is built in a logical order, which will help you better understand the material. There are also the following features:

Exercises   These are hands-on examples of how to use GitHub Copilot.

Exam Essentials   This section summarizes the key points, concepts, and topics of the chapter. You should be able to perform each of the tasks or convey the information requested.

Review Questions   There are 20 multiple choice questions at the end of each chapter. You should answer these questions and check your answers against the ones provided after the questions. If you can't answer at least 80 percent of these questions correctly, go back and review the chapter, or at least those sections that seem to be giving you difficulty.

Interactive Online Learning Environment and Test Bank

This book is accompanied by an online learning environment that provides several additional elements. Items available among these companion files include the following:

Practice Tests   All the questions from the book are included on a proprietary digital test engine—including the 28-question assessment test at the end of this Introduction and the 140 questions that make up the review question sections at the end of each chapter. In addition, there is a 65-question bonus exam.

Electronic "Flashcards"   The digital companion files include 100 questions in flashcard format (a question followed by a single correct answer).

Glossary   The key terms from this book, and their definitions, are available as a fully searchable PDF.

Interactive Online Learning Environment and Test Bank

You can access all these resources at www.wiley.com/go/sybextestprep.

GitHub does provide its own tutorials, which you can find at https://learn .microsoft.com/en-us/training/paths/copilot/?wt.mc_id=github_ inproduct_copilotfoundations_mslearn_ghcertregistration.

There is also the Copilot documentation. It is located at https://docs.github. com/en/copilot.

But again, the book has all the material you need.

How This Book Is Organized

This book consists of seven chapters:

Chapter 1, "The Fundamentals of AI and Its Responsible Use," covers technologies like deep learning, generative AI, and large language models (LLMs). There is also an overview of the core principles of responsible AI, including fairness, reliability and safety, privacy and security, inclusiveness, transparency, and accountability.

Chapter 2, "Introduction to GitHub Copilot," describes the pros and cons of this powerful tool, including use cases and capabilities. These include GitHub Copilot Chat, slash commands, code completion, and Edits.

Chapter 3, "Differences in GitHub Copilot Versions," focuses on the four plans for GitHub Copilot. The main differences include audit logs, pull request summaries, and custom models.

Chapter 4, "The Role of Data," covers how GitHub Copilot and LLMs work with data. There is an overview of how prompts are processed, which involves prompt engineering, model processing, post processing, and safety.

Chapter 5, "Prompt Crafting and Engineering," explains the best practices for creating prompts for GitHub Copilot. Specific approaches include zero-and few-shot learning, asking for alternatives, and chain-of-thought (CoT) prompting.

Chapter 6, "Developer Use Cases for GitHub Copilot," describes many ways you can use GitHub Copilot. Topics include learning languages, creating documentation, using code refactoring, generating data, and debugging.

Chapter 7, "Testing and Privacy Considerations," describes how to use GitHub Copilot to create unit and integration tests. There is also an overview of different approaches for providing for privacy, such as with content exclusions and policy management.

Exam Objectives

The GitHub Copilot Certification Study Guide has been written to cover every exam objective at a level appropriate to its exam weighting. The following table provides a breakdown of this book's exam coverage, showing you the weight of each section and the chapter where each objective or subobjective is covered:

Subject Area	Percent of Exam
Domain 1: Responsible AI	7%
Domain 2: GitHub Copilot plans and features	31%
Domain 3: How GitHub Copilot works and handles data	15%
Domain 4: Prompt crafting and prompt engineering	9%
Domain 5: Developer use cases for AI	14%
Domain 6: Testing with GitHub Copilot	9%
Domain 7: Privacy fundamentals and context exclusions	15%
Total	100%

Objective Map

Domain 1: Responsible AI

Explain Responsible Usage of AI

Exam Objective	Chapter
Describe the risks associated with using AI	1
Explain the limitations of using generative AI tools (dept of the source data for the model, bias in the data, etc.)	1
Explain the need to validate the output of AI tools	1
- Identify how to operate a responsible AI	1
- Identify the potential harms of generative AI (bias, secure code, fairness, privacy, transparency)	1
Explain how to mitigate the occurrence of potential harms	1
- Explain ethical AI	1

Domain 2: GitHub Copilot Plans and Features

Identify the Different GitHub Copilot Plans

Exam Objective	Chapter
Understand the differences between Copilot Individual, Copilot Business, Copilot Enterprise, and Copilot Business for non-GHE	2
Understand Copilot for non-GitHub customers	2
Define GitHub Copilot in the IDE	2
Define GitHub Copilot Chat in the IDE	2
Describe the different ways to trigger GitHub Copilot (chat, inline chat, suggestions, multiple suggestions, exception handling, CLI)	2

Identify the Main Features with GitHub Copilot Chat

Exam Objective	Chapter
Identify the use cases where GitHub Copilot Chat is most effective	2
Explain how to improve performance for GitHub Copilot Chat	2
Identify the limitations of using GitHub Copilot Chat	2
Identify the available options for using code suggestions from GitHub Copilot Chat	2
Explain how to share feedback about GitHub Copilot Chat	2
Identify the common best practices for using GitHub Copilot Chat	2
Identify the available slash commands when using GitHub Copilot Chat	2

Using GitHub Copilot in the CLI

Exam Objective	Chapter
Discuss the steps for installing GitHub Copilot in the CLI	2
Identify the common commands when using GitHub Copilot in the CLI	2
Identify the multiple settings you can configure within GitHub Copilot in the CLI	2

Identify the Main Features with GitHub Copilot Individual

Exam Objective	Chapter
Explain the difference between GitHub Copilot Individual and GitHub Copilot Business (data exclusions, IP indemnity, billing, etc.)	3
Understand the available features in the IDE for GitHub Copilot Individual	3

Identify the Main Features of GitHub Copilot Business

Exam Objective	Chapter
Demonstrate how to exclude specific files from GitHub Copilot	3
Demonstrate how to establish organization-wide policy management	3
Describe the purpose of organization audit logs for GitHub Copilot Business	3
Explain how to search audit log events for GitHub Copilot Business	3
Explain how to manage GitHub Copilot Business subscriptions via the REST API	3

Identify the Main Features with GitHub Copilot Enterprise

Exam Objective	Chapter
Explain the benefits of using GitHub Copilot Chat on GitHub.com	3
Explain GitHub Copilot pull request summaries	3
Explain how to configure and use Knowledge Bases within GitHub Copilot Enterprise	3
Describe the different types of knowledge that can be stored in a Knowledge Base (e.g. code snippets, best practices, design patterns)	3
Explain the benefits of using Knowledge Bases for code completion and review (e.g. improve code quality, consistency, and efficiency)	3
Describe instructions for creating, managing, and searching Knowledge Bases within GitHub Copilot Enterprise, including details on indexing and other relevant configuration steps	3
Explain the benefits of using custom models	3

Domain 3: How GitHub Copilot Works and Handles Data

Describe How GitHub Copilot Handles Data

Exam Objective	Chapter
Describe how the data in GitHub Copilot individual is used and shared	4
Explain the data flow for GitHub Copilot code completion	4
Explain the data flow for GitHub Copilot Chat	4
Describe the different types of input processing for GitHub Copilot Chat (types of prompts it was designed for)	4

Describe the Data Pipeline Lifecycle of GitHub Copilot Code Suggestions in the IDE

Exam Objective	Chapter
Visualize the lifecycle of a GitHub Copilot code suggestion	4
Explain how GitHub Copilot gathers context	4
Explain how GitHub Copilot builds a prompt	4
Describe the proxy service and the filters each prompt goes through	4
Describe how the large language model produces its response	4
Explain the post-processing of GitHub Copilot's responses through the proxy server	4
Identify how GitHub Copilot identifies matching code	4

Describe the Limitations of GitHub Copilot (and LLMs in General)

Exam Objective	Chapter
Describe the effect of most seen examples on the source data	4
Describe the age of code suggestions (how old and relevant the data is)	4
Describe the nature of GitHub Copilot providing reasoning and context from a prompt vs calculations	4
Describe the limited context window	4

Domain 4: Prompt Crafting and Prompt Engineering

Describe the Fundamentals of Prompt Crafting

Describe the Fundamentals of Prompt Crafting

Domain 5: Developer Use Cases for AI

Improve Developer Productivity AI

- Learning new programming languages and frameworks
- Language translation
- Context switching
- Writing documentation
- Personalized context-aware responses
- Generating sample data
- Modernizing legacy applications
- Debugging code
- Data science
- Code refactoring

Domain 6: Testing with GitHub Copilot

Describe the Options for Generating Testing for Your Code

Enhance Code Quality Through Testing

Leverage GitHub Copilot for Security and Performance

Domain 7: Privacy Fundamentals and Context Exclusions

Describe the Different SKUs for GitHub Copilot

Identify Content Exclusions

Safeguards

Troubleshooting

Assessment Test

1. What is a reason a generative AI tool like GitHub Copilot might create low-quality code?

    A. It uses private codebases as training data.

    B. Sometimes the underlying dataset for the model is low quality.

    C. It has difficulties with common programming languages.

    D. There is not enough labeled data.

2. Which of the following is a way to protect privacy in an AI system?

    A. Make data public in a repository

    B. Use only old data to avoid personal information

    C. Encrypt and anonymize data

    D. Only rely on automated safety filters

3. How can you improve fairness in an AI system?

    A. Only use AI systems for non-sensitive tasks

    B. Focus on small datasets

    C. Use proprietary datasets

    D. Use a diverse team and review datasets

4. What is a hallucination?

    A. When an AI system fails to generate a response

    B. When AI generates a response that is slow

    C. When AI creates false or misleading information

    D. When the AI system has reached the limit for processing data

5. What is required for using GitHub Copilot in VS Code?

    A. An encryption key

    B. A GitHub account and the Copilot extension

    C. A paid subscription only

    D. A Docker container

6. For GitHub Copilot, what is a chat variable?

    A. A way to select an LLM

    B. A keyboard shortcut

    C. A way to provide context in a prompt

    D. A security setting

7. Which IDE has the highest degree of integration with GitHub Copilot?

    A. Xcode

    B. Vim

    C. JetBrains

    D. VS Code

8. In GitHub Copilot Chat, what does `@workspace` do?

    A. Connects to your Git history

    B. Creates the files for a new project

    C. Analyzes the structure of your project's code

    D. Allows for using AI in the terminal window

9. What do you need to use the Enterprise version of GitHub Copilot?

    A. The OpenAI API

    B. A GitHub Enterprise Cloud subscription

    C. An organization with a minimum of five seats

    D. The GitHub Copilot REST API

10. When using GitHub Copilot, what happens if a suggestion matches public code?

    A. It is deleted.

    B. The code is sent to the GitHub Security Hub.

    C. A notification is shown with license information.

    D. There is an automatic security review.

11. What is a reason to use the GitHub Copilot REST API?

    A. To build mobile backends

    B. To use third-party extensions

    C. To configure security notifications

    D. To automate seat and policy management

12. What is the main reason to use slash commands in GitHub Copilot?

    A. To delete code from a code file

    B. To customize AI models

    C. To give instructions in Chat

    D. To manage billing and subscriptions

13. How does telemetry data help GitHub Copilot?

    A. It helps with authentication.

    B. It improves code quality by matching similar code repositories.

    C. It provides user feedback.

    D. It is used to select an AI model.

14. What is the purpose of the safety filter in GitHub Copilot?

    A. To check for security risks and responsible AI practices

    B. To identify syntax errors

    C. To fix logic errors

    D. To add error handling to code

15. What is a disadvantage of GitHub Copilot's context window?

    A. It limits the number of suggestions each month.

    B. It can only be used with OpenAI models.

    C. It only works with Python.

    D. It can only process a certain amount of code at one time.

16. How does GitHub Copilot gather context for code suggestions?

    A. By accessing similar GitHub repositories

    B. By requiring uploading files into GitHub Copilot

    C. By analyzing the active file, related files, and metadata

    D. By using telemetry data

17. Why might a prompt generate a poor response from GitHub Copilot?

    A. There is not a reference to a coding style guide.

    B. The prompt is too short.

    C. The prompt is too vague or confusing.

    D. The prompt does not use slash commands.

18. Which programming language options are available for GitHub Copilot?

    A. GitHub Copilot only works with Python, JavaScript, and Java.

    B. GitHub Copilot supports many programming languages from its training data.

    C. GitHub Copilot requires uploading programming language modules.

    D. GitHub Copilot only allows for scripting languages.

19. In what way does GitHub Copilot use Chat history for generating responses?

    A. It only looks at the last Chat response.

    B. It does not use the Chat history.

    C. It uses the Chat history to improve the accuracy and relevance of the response.

    D. It archives it to a repository for compliance purposes.

20. For the prompt process flow in GitHub Copilot, what follows after analyzing the context?

    A. The LLM generates code snippets.

    B. The system generates a user feedback report.

    C. A different AI model is used.

    D. A prompt is formed using context, recent edits, and Chat history.

21. What is the purpose of decomposing conditionals when refactoring code with GitHub Copilot?

    A. To delete legacy logic

    B. To convert code to another language

    C. To break down complex decisions into smaller functions

    D. To make the code optimized for mobile devices

22. How can GitHub Copilot generate sample data?

    A. By connecting to a third-party relational database

    B. By using a custom AI model

    C. By importing data from government sites

    D. By using a prompt to generate realistic test data like user IDs and passwords

23. In what way does GitHub Copilot reduce the problem of context switching for developers?

    A. It removes all project dependencies.

    B. It stores full system logs automatically.

    C. It integrates directly into code editors like VS Code and JetBrains.

    D. It blocks external API calls.

24. Which of the following is a way to generate tests using GitHub Copilot?

    A. Use the `/unittest` slash command.

    B. Ask GitHub Copilot to run the code automatically.

    C. Use the `/tests` slash command or custom prompts.

    D. Install a third-party plugin for testing.

25. How can GitHub Copilot help with writing assertions in a test?

   A. By suggesting appropriate assertion statements based on the function's behavior

   B. By using a testing library

   C. By creating random outputs

   D. By using a third-party extension

26. Which of the following is a security best practice that GitHub Copilot might recommend?

   A. Using fewer functions in your code

   B. Storing passwords in plain text for easier debugging

   C. Validating user input to prevent injection attacks

   D. Removing error messages from logs

27. What is an impact of allowing content exclusions at the organization level in GitHub Copilot Enterprise?

   A. It prevents selected files or paths from being used to generate Copilot suggestions.

   B. It removes private repositories from GitHub.

   C. It disables Copilot suggestions.

   D. It forces all repositories to become read-only.

28. What is the purpose of the duplication detector filter in GitHub Copilot?

   A. To provide disaster recovery if there is a failure

   B. To detect and block suggestions that closely match public code

   C. To run code performance benchmarks

   D. To remove comments from the code

Note

1. Stackoverflow.com (May 2024). Stack Overflow's 2024 Developer Survey. https://survey.stack overflow.co/2024/ai/ (accessed 18 March 2025).

Answers to Assessment Test

1.   B. Generative AI models for software development are trained on huge amounts of code from public repositories, such as GitHub. However, there may be low quality code. This can result in code generation that may be verbose or difficult to maintain. For more information, see Chapter 1, "The Fundamentals of AI and Its Responsible Use."

2.   C. GitHub recommends that privacy should be protected by encrypting and anonymizing data. For more information, see Chapter 1, "The Fundamentals of AI and Its Responsible Use."

3.   D. Microsoft recommends having diverse teams develop AI models. There should also be regular human reviews. For more information, see Chapter 1, "The Fundamentals of AI and Its Responsible Use."

4.   C. A hallucination is where an AI system generates false or misleading responses. This is due to the complexities of the transformer model and the quality of the underlying dataset. For more information, see Chapter 1, "The Fundamentals of AI and Its Responsible Use."

5.   B. Before you can use GitHub Copilot in VS Code, you need a GitHub account—which can be the free version—and the Copilot extension, which is available in the marketplace. For more information, see Chapter 2, "Introduction to GitHub Copilot."

6.   C. A chat variable starts with the # character, such as #file or #editor. They provide more context in your prompt, which allows for an improved response. For more information, see Chapter 2, "Introduction to GitHub Copilot."

7.   D. With VS Code, you get the most up-to-date version of GitHub Copilot. This is the recommended IDE for this tool. For more information, see Chapter 2, "Introduction to GitHub Copilot."

8.   C. The @workspace is what you use in a prompt. It references the structure and code files in your project. This helps generate better suggestions, explanations, and code. For more information, see Chapter 2, "Introduction to GitHub Copilot."

9.   B. To use GitHub Copilot Enterprise, you need the paid GitHub Enterprise Cloud subscription. You cannot use a trial version. For more information, see Chapter 3, "Differences in GitHub Copilot Versions."

10.   C. If the generated code from GitHub Copilot matches public code—such as from a repository—you will be notified. There will be information about the source and license details. For more information, see Chapter 3, "Differences in GitHub Copilot Versions."

11.   D. The REST API is available for the Business and Enterprise editions. It allows for automating tasks, such for managing user seats and retrieving usage data. For more information, see Chapter 3, "Differences in GitHub Copilot Versions."

12. C. Slash commands are short instructions you use in Chat, such as to generate, debug or explain code. For more information, see Chapter 3, "Differences in GitHub Copilot Versions."

13. C. Telemetry data is information about what suggestions users accept or reject. This data is used to improve the AI models. For more information, see Chapter 4, "The Role of Data."

14. A. The safety filter in GitHub Copilot is used to identify risky code and to ensure responsible AI guidelines. For more information, see Chapter 4, "The Role of Data."

15. D. The AI models used in GitHub Copilot have context windows. This means that these systems can only analyze a limited amount of code at a time. For more information, see Chapter 4, "The Role of Data."

16. C. Context provides more information for a prompt, so as to generate a better response. GitHub will collect data from the current file, other open tabs, and use metadata. For more information, see Chapter 4, "The Role of Data."

17. C. Generally, prompts need to be clear and provide enough context. If not, the AI system can misunderstand what is being asked. For more information, see Chapter 5, "Prompt Crafting and Engineering."

18. B. GitHub has not disclosed the number of languages supported. But there are, nonetheless, many supported. The reason is that they are based on large amounts of public repositories. For more information, see Chapter 5, "Prompt Crafting and Engineering."

19. C. GitHub Copilot uses the Chat history as a way to better understand the context of a prompt. This should help provide more accurate and useful responses. For more information, see Chapter 5, "Prompt Crafting and Engineering."

20. D. Once GitHub Copilot has gathered the context, it will create a prompt that includes information such as code, edits, and Chat history. For more information, see Chapter 5, "Prompt Crafting and Engineering."

21. C. The decomposing of conditions is about splitting large decision blocks into smaller, clearer functions. This helps improve readability and maintainability of the code. For more information, see Chapter 6, "Developer Use Cases for GitHub Copilot."

22. D. GitHub Copilot can generate realistic sample data, such as test usernames and passwords. You can also do this in formats like JSON or CSV. For more information, see Chapter 6, "Developer Use Cases for GitHub Copilot."

23. C. GitHub Copilot reduces context switching by providing in-editor code suggestions and explanations. This helps developers stay focused on their work. For more information, see Chapter 6, "Developer Use Cases for GitHub Copilot."

24. C. For creating tests, you can use the `/tests` slash command or create a custom prompt, which can provide more detail. For more information, see Chapter 7, "Testing and Privacy Considerations."

25. A. GitHub Copilot will analyze the code, so as to detect the patterns. From this, it will generate assertion statements to test a function's expected output. For more information, see Chapter 7, "Testing and Privacy Considerations."

26. C. When you do a code review, GitHub Copilot will provide suggestions based on security best practices, such as validating user inputs to prevent vulnerabilities like injection attacks. For more information, see Chapter 7, "Testing and Privacy Considerations."

27. A. When you set content exclusions at the organization level, GitHub Copilot will be restricted from using specific files or directories when generating code suggestions. This helps improve security and privacy. For more information, see Chapter 7, "Testing and Privacy Considerations."

28. B. In GitHub Copilot, the duplication detector will filter for identical or nearly identical code from public repositories. This helps avoid intellectual property infringement. For more information, see Chapter 7, "Testing and Privacy Considerations."

Chapter

1

The Fundamentals of AI and Its Responsible Use

THE GITHUB COPILOT EXAM OBJECTIVES COVERED IN THIS CHAPTER INCLUDE, BUT ARE NOT LIMITED TO, THE FOLLOWING:

✔ **Domain 1: Responsible AI**

- Explain responsible usage of AI

  - Describe the risks associated with using AI

  - Explain the limitations of using generative AI tools (dept of the source data for the model, bias in the data, etc.)

  - Explain the need to validate the output of AI tools

  - Identify how to operate a responsible AI

  - Identify the potential harms of generative AI (bias, secure code, fairness, privacy, transparency)

  - Explain how to mitigate the occurrence of potential harms

  - Explain ethical AI

The goal of this chapter is to give you a broad overview of artificial intelligence (AI) and to set a solid foundation.

The first few sections of the book, though, are not covered on the exam. They include the principles of AI coding, the abstraction of programming languages, and the basics of AI. Yet these are important to cover since they make some of the exam-focused topics easier to understand.

The chapter also covers areas that are relevant to the exam, such as the risks of generative AI—including topics like hallucinations and bias—and responsible AI. It also looks at how AI coding systems can use different models.

Finally, the chapter covers a few other topics that are not on the exam but are still helpful in learning about some of the powerful features of GitHub Copilot, such as using different AI models. The chapter talks about how AI coding is reshaping traditional development and evaluates some of the alternatives to GitHub Copilot.

AI Coding and GitHub Copilot

AI coding is about using AI for writing, testing, and debugging code. It's one of the most dynamic areas of technology, as it seems like every day there is a new innovation. It can be difficult to keep up with everything.

Regardless, AI coding is quickly becoming mainstream. Here's what Hadi Partovi, CEO of Code.org, had to say about it[1]:

> "At this point, software engineering without AI is a little bit like writing without a word processor."

Or consider this tweet from Paul Graham, cofounder of Y Combinator[2]:

> "I met a 19 year old yesterday who'd been using AI to write code since he was 16. It was not an advance to him. It was just how programming is done. He took it for granted that AI will eventually write most code."

To get a sense of the pervasiveness of AI coding, look at Google. The company, which has about 60,000 developers, generates more than a quarter of its code using AI.[3] This was according to a statement from CEO Sundar Pichai in late 2024.[4] It seems like a good bet that this percentage will continue to grow.

One of the leading AI coding tools is *GitHub Copilot*, which was launched in June 2021.[5] This came about 17 months before the introduction of ChatGPT. GitHub used a specialized AI model, called Codex, that was customized for coding tasks. The system was essentially a derivative of OpenAI's GPT-3 model.

While this was an early generation of the model, GitHub Copilot was still quite powerful. Andrej Karpathy, founding member of OpenAI and entrepreneur, tweeted this about it[6]:

> "Copilot has dramatically accelerated my coding; it's hard to imagine going back to 'manual coding.' Still learning to use it but it already writes ~80 percent of my code, ~80 percent accuracy. I don't even really code, I prompt and edit."

Soon after, other AI-coding tools sprang up. Some were from startups like Cursor, others from mega-tech companies, such as Amazon and Google. But GitHub has remained the top player.

There are many reasons for this. The system is a first mover. GitHub also has a massive userbase, many talented developers, a strong AI team, and a willingness to focus on innovation.

All in all, learning GitHub Copilot is a smart decision, and getting the certification is a way to help you stand out.

Programming Languages and Abstraction

Abstraction is about simplifying complex systems, which is critical for software development. You do not want a project to get bogged down in unnecessary technical details. A developer should also not have to understand the inner workings of every component. As much as possible, a developer should be able to focus on higher-level concepts, which helps speed up development and improve quality. Abstraction also makes it easier to maintain and adapt codebases.

As should be no surprise, abstraction is a major driver for the evolution of programming languages. For example, the first ones were highly cryptic and prone to error. They used machine language, which consisted of long strings of binary digits or 0s and 1s.

But there would quickly emerge abstractions, such as assembly language. True, this was still complex. Then again, assembly language did use characters!

It would not be until the 1950s that we saw the emergence of high-level languages, which used human-readable syntax. Some examples included Fortran and COBOL. In fact, COBOL was written in a way that allowed nontechnical people to understand the workflows. This was important since this language was mostly about business applications that were often audited by accountants and business analysts.

After this, languages started to adopt more structured approaches. They involved using *functions* and *subroutines*. This would eventually be followed by *object-oriented programming*. With these approaches, software code became more modular and reusable.

However, the leveraging of AI for software development has represented perhaps the most transformative level of abstraction. You no longer write code. Instead, you write *prompts*— that is, natural language instructions. As Karpathy has tweeted[7]:

> "The hottest new programming language is English."

This is not to imply you do not have to understand software languages. You still do. The main reason is that AI coding systems sometimes generate code that has bugs.

You'll also need to understand how to craft effective prompts—known as *prompt engineering*. They will allow you to get the most from an AI coding system.

The Basics of AI

Defining AI can be a challenge. It's a complicated technology and is constantly undergoing change. The industry also has much hype and marketing exaggerations.

But a helpful way of understanding AI is to use a diagram, which you can see in Figure 1.1.

FIGURE 1.1   The different forms of AI.

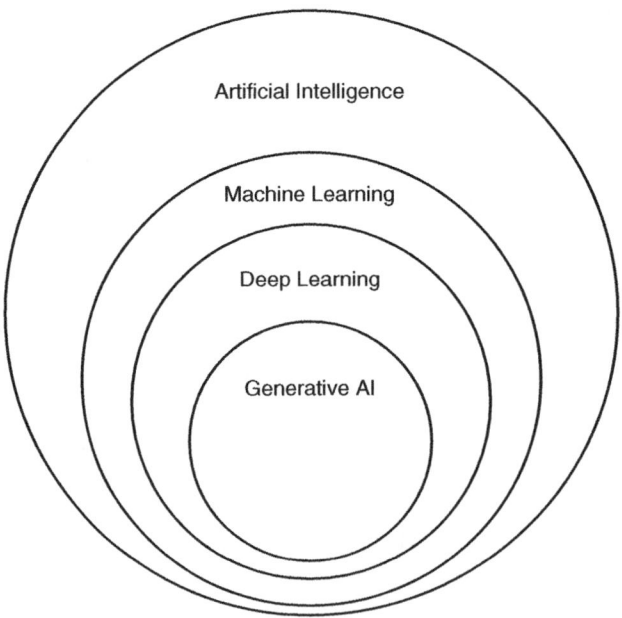

Basically, AI is a general term that includes various types of technologies like *machine learning* (ML), *deep learning* (DL) and *generative AI* (GenAI). For the most part, they allow machines to engage in learning, reasoning, problem solving, and decision-making.

Machine Learning (ML)

Machine learning (ML) is one of the earliest approaches to AI. In 1959, IBM researcher Arthur Samuel published a paper that set forth the elements of this technology.[8] The basic idea was that ML allows a computer to learn without being explicitly programmed. In the paper, Samuel noted:

> "Programming computers to learn from experience should eventually eliminate the need for much of this detailed programming effort."

To understand ML, let's take an example of a spam filtering application. To create one, you need large amounts of data. This includes emails that are labeled either "spam" or "not spam." You then train this model using an available ML algorithm, like *linear regression, decision trees,* or *k-nearest neighbors.* A popular one for spam detection is the *Naive Bayes Classifier.* This uses probability analysis to determine the likelihood of an email being spam.

Once the ML model is trained, it will be fed emails in a person's email program. Any spam will then be sent to a separate folder.

But an effective ML model needs monitoring and updates. For example, Gmail will improve its models by using user feedback, such as when a person marks emails as spam or not.

This process is known as *labeling data.* When an ML model uses this approach, it is called *supervised learning.* This is usually for classification, which divides data into classes or categories. Besides spam filtering applications, other examples of this include image recognition and fraud detection.

But supervised learning is also used with regression. This where labeled data predicts numerical values, such as temperatures or home prices.

Besides supervised learning, there are two other ways ML can help a computer learn:

- *Unsupervised learning*: This uses unlabeled data. For this, an ML algorithm will find patterns in groups or clusters. A scenario for this is a product recommendation system. For example, if a customer buys a book about cooking, the system might predict that they are likely to buy kitchen gadgets or other cookbooks.

- *Reinforcement learning*: This trains a model based on rewards and punishments when there is interaction with an environment. An example is game playing. Reinforcement learning can improve performance by going through many moves and seeing which ones result in the highest scores.

Deep Learning (DL)

Deep learning (DL) is a subset of ML. The core technology has origins that go back to the 1950s, with the introduction of neural networks. They were inspired by the human brain. A neural network involves nodes or "neurons" that are connected to each other. Through this, a machine can learn by analyzing the patterns in data.

As for DL, it is a much more complex neural network that can process large amounts of data. You generally use this for classification tasks.

Figure 1.2 shows a simple diagram of a DL model.

To see how a DL model works, suppose you want to predict customer churn for a product. This is the rate that customers stop using a product or service over a specific period of time.

First, you need to collect labeled data. For this, a customer account will be labeled as to whether there has been churn or not. You also need other variables or *features*, such as income levels, location, subscription plan, frequency of product use, number of support tickets, payment history, and so on.

Once you have the data, you prepare it for the input layer of the DL model. This includes steps like cleaning up the data for gaps, errors, and outliers. The data will then need to be converted into *vectors*, which are strings of numbers that the model can process. An example is shown in Figure 1.3.

Each row is for a customer, and each column is for the features. The vector is fed into the input layer. In the diagram in Figure 1.2, the circles represent neurons or nodes.

When the vectors are fed into the input layer of the DL model, this will start a process for predicting whether a customer will churn or not. This is known as *forward propagation.*

In this process, the next step is the processing with the hidden layer. This is where the DL model learns. The vectors will be multiplied by weights and added with biases (or constants). These are also known as *parameters.*

FIGURE 1.2 A simple deep learning model.

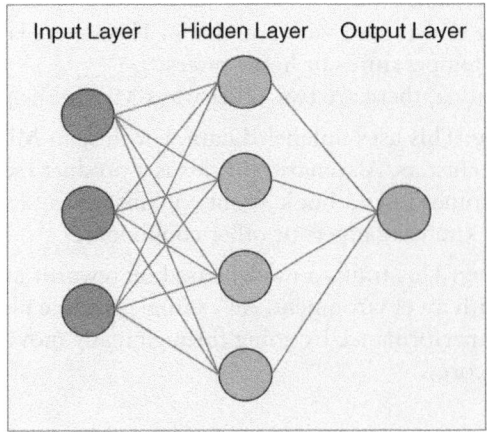

Input Layer   Hidden Layer   Output Layer

FIGURE 1.3   A vector for a DL model.

$$X = \begin{bmatrix} 0 & 3 & 10 & 0.1 & 1 & 0.2 & 0 \\ 1 & 0 & 5 & 0.6 & 0 & 0.8 & 1 \\ 0 & 2 & 8 & 0.3 & 1 & 0.4 & 0 \end{bmatrix}$$

Then an *activation function* will be used, which will ignore negative values. For complex models, there can be hundreds of hidden layers. Through this process, the DL model will recognize patterns. For example, if a feature shows that a customer has high usage, then the weight will be lower for the risk of churn. The opposite is true if there are many support tickets.

The adjusted values for the vectors are fed into the output layer. This is the prediction for the model that is based on a function. In this case, it could be a *sigmoid function* because there is one output. It's a probability from 0 to 1 to indicate the likelihood of churn.

Suppose that the model predicts there's a 90 percent probability of churn for a customer, but this proves to be wrong. This is where *backpropagation* comes in to the DL process. This begins by using a loss function to measure the size of the error. Then the DL model works backward, layer by layer. This involves evaluating the weights, attempting to find where there is too much or too little. This iteration process may happen thousands of times until it narrows on a better prediction.

While the past decade has seen continued advances in DL, the overall structure of the technology has remained the same. This has resulted in incredible innovations. Just some include self-driving cars, facial recognition, and disease prediction.

DL has also been critical for AI coding systems. But the key advancement has been generative AI, which is built on DL models.

Generative AI (GenAI)

Generative AI (GenAI) is at the heart of AI coding systems. This technology allows for creating and understanding content, whether text, voice, images, or video.

GenAI is fairly new. The origins go back to a paper published in 2017, entitled "Attention Is All You Need."[9] Most of the authors were from Google Research.

They proposed a revolutionary new approach—called the *transformer model*—to understand language. Before this, a model would often use recurrent neural networks (RNNs). These analyzed one word at a time, which was slow and often failed to grasp the overall context of text.

What the transformer did was use so-called *attention mechanisms*. They allowed for processing of words as a whole.

This type of model—which is often referred to as a *large language model* (LLM)—is also trained on enormous amounts of data. In cases of state-of-the-art models from companies like OpenAI and Anthropic, this likely includes most of the information on the Internet. This is why a model can seem to answer any question—and do so with human-like language.

No doubt, the transformer model is highly complex and involves advanced math. But the overall structure is actually straightforward.

Take a look at an example. This will be for the *inference* of the transformer, which is how it processes input from a user and generates content.

Suppose you use a chatbot and enter the following prompt:

Use Python to calculate the Fibonacci sequence.

Here are the steps for processing the transformer model:

- *Tokenization*: This involves splitting sentences into tokens, which are numbers. A *token* represents a word, part of a word, a character, or punctuation. In this example, the word "Use"—along with the following space—could be one token, "Python" could be one token, and so on. A rule of thumb is that for every 700 to 750 words there are about 1,000 tokens.

- *Embeddings*: The tokens are converted into embeddings by using a neural network. These are vectors that show the similarities between the words. By doing this, the transformer model can better understand that "Python" is a programming language, not a snake. This is done by understanding the surrounding words, like "function" and "calculate."

- *Positional encoding*: The embedding process will change the order of the tokens. But this can mean losing the meaning of the text. By using positional encoding, the tokens are placed in the original positions.

- *Multi-head self-attention*: This uses neural networks to understand what tokens to focus on. It's done by multiple layers of feed-forward steps to improve the results. The process will essentially use sophisticated probability analysis to predict the next most likely tokens. In this example, the prompt will predict that there should be content for creating a Python function that calculates a Fibonacci sequence.

What this means is that the transformer model does not actually have inherent knowledge. Instead, it is essentially a prediction machine. However, since it is based on a large dataset, it can seem like the model knows what it is processing.

Regardless, the transformer model has been shown to be highly effective for code generation. There are some reasons for this:

- **Data:** There is huge amounts of coding data available from the Internet, say from Stack Overflow, GitHub, and many blogs. This is especially the case with popular languages like Python, Java, and C. In other words, when you prompt an LLM about how to code a task, the transformer model will likely have information about it. In fact, it may have seen thousands of examples of certain types of code.

- **Structure:** Programming languages are highly structured, which makes it easier for the transformer model. It means that there is not as much variability with the probability analysis. This helps reduce errors. But the prediction capability is also important with autocomplete, since this is about predicting the most likely next word.

- **Attention:** This aspect of the transformer model allows for more relevant code generation. For example, if you want to write a function, it will focus more on elements like the signature and arguments. But the attention will also recognize other relevant information, such as a variable that is mentioned earlier.

- **Debugging:** The transformer model's logical and structured approach helps with this process. It can identify bugs by analyzing the likely steps in a routine. With attention, it can also take into account surrounding information.

The Risks and Drawbacks of GenAI

While GenAI models are incredibly powerful, there are clear disadvantages. The technology is far from a silver bullet.

There are a large number of technology luminaries who think that GenAI poses existential threats. In an open letter published in March 2023, prominent technology leaders and researchers called for a temporary halt in development of GenAI systems.[10] They feared there was not enough oversight and that the technology could lead to unintended consequences, such as job displacement, disinformation, and even loss of control over mission-critical systems. Some of the signatories were Steve Wozniak, Yuval Noah Harari, and Elon Musk.

Granted, this seemed more like something out of science fiction, like Skynet from the dystopian movie *The Terminator*. Would GenAI really go against humanity?

Since the letter was published, the concerns do seem overblown. Part of this has been the exaggeration of the powers of AI systems. Another reason is that AI applications, such as chatbots, have implemented strong safeguards and security. Yet this does not mean that there aren't clear risks and issues with GenAI.

Some of these include the following:

- Hallucinations
- Bias
- Security threats
- Black box concerns
- Low-quality code
- Limited context windows
- Recency problem
- High costs

This section takes a closer look at each of these.

Hallucinations

A *hallucination* is when an LLM generates false or misleading content. This happens because the underlying data may be sparse or incorrect. As a result, the GenAI predicts the wrong information. Moreover, LLMs usually do not have real-time systems to correct the problems.

For an AI coding system, hallucinations may often be more of an inconvenience. The reason is that your compiler should be able to handle the obvious syntax and logic errors.

Instead, the real problem is when the GenAI generates code that is functionally correct but has underlying issues. Here are some examples:

- Flawed calculations or algorithms
- Loops that iterate too few or too many times
- Conditional logic that leads to the wrong paths
- Using operations on the wrong data
- Exception handling that is too broad or too narrow
- Regular expressions that have the wrong formatting

In some cases, the LLM may create frameworks that do not exist. Or, it may make up configurations or capabilities.

Keep in mind that there have been considerable strides in mitigating hallucinations in GenAI systems. There has been a lot of academic research in this category. Many AI companies have also invested heavily in this area.

Another way to deal with hallucinations is to customize LLMs. There are several techniques for this. One is *fine-tuning*, which means including proprietary data—say internal source code—in the LLM. This is done by changing the parameters of the model. However, this is complicated and time-consuming, requiring advanced data science skills.

Another approach that is simpler is *retrieval augmented generation* (RAG). This also connects a proprietary dataset to an LLM. But this is done by using a search algorithm.

Despite all these efforts, hallucinations continue to be an ongoing problem. This is why it's important that you always review code that's generated from an AI coding system.

Bias

According to the Merriam-Webster dictionary, *bias* is "a personal and sometimes unreasoned judgment: prejudice."[11] Unfortunately, AI can reflect this in its content.

There are different ways this happens:

- **Data collection:** This is generally the most common way that bias seeps into an AI system. Simply put, the dataset will often reflect the prejudices or stereotypes of society.
- **Data labeling:** If this is done by people, their own views can skew the creation and application of the labels for the dataset.

- **Model training:** The developer of a model may be influenced by their own biases. This can happen with the design of the parameters.

This is not to imply that AI professionals are inherently prejudicial. It's often the case that bias is unconscious. This is called *implicit bias*. Let's face it, people usually do not want to be prejudiced or to hold stereotypes. They want to do the right thing.

However, in some cases, a person does intend to be prejudiced. This is called *explicit bias*.

Regardless, bias can be difficult to detect and manage. Part of this is due to cultural differences. For example, the views of someone in China may be different from someone who has grown up in the United States, Europe, or Africa.

Yet bias can lead to serious consequences. It can increase discrimination, affecting hiring practices, lending decisions, or even criminal justice.

It's impossible to completely eliminate bias. Even the best systems have it. The key is finding ways to mitigate the level of bias in an AI application.

Here are some approaches:

- **Training:** Periodic classes, workshops, or videos for the AI team can be helpful in reducing bias.

- **Data preparation:** In this process, cleaning data helps reduce the bias. But there should also be a proactive effort to spot the signs. There should also be a focus on using datasets that are not skewed toward certain demographics.

- **Ethics frameworks:** These are guidelines or polices for handling bias. There are many available. Later in this chapter, we look at a framework from Microsoft.

- **Auditing and monitoring:** When an AI application is in production, there should be systems to log potential issues of bias.

There are also tools to help identify and address biases, such as:

- **AI Fairness 360:** This is an open-source project backed by IBM. It provides systems for detecting and mitigating bias.

- **What-If Tool:** This is a tool from Google. It has an intuitive interface that makes it easier to analyze bias in AI models.

- **Fairlearn:** This is an open-source software project from Microsoft. It is a sophisticated system for bias detection and correction.

The developers of AI coding tools also continue to invest in methods and best practices for reducing bias. This is especially the case with GitHub Copilot. The fact that responsible AI is part of the GitHub Copilot exam is a validation of this.

Despite all this, AI coding systems still have much to do. Take a look at a research paper entitled "Bias Testing and Mitigation in LLM-based Code Generation."[12] It highlights that LLMs can produce code containing biases about age, gender, and race. An evaluation of five leading LLMs showed that 20.29 to 44.93 percent of the generated code functions were biased when handling tasks involving sensitive attributes.

Security Threats

AI coding systems are vulnerable to security threats. For example, when you use an LLM, your data will usually be sent to the cloud. This is why you should be careful about the data you input into a system. You should make sure this meets your security requirements.

Next, an LLM can sometimes create insecure code. Here are some examples:

- **Injections:** This is code that allows for the execution of unauthorized commands. There are various methods. One is a *SQL injection*. This is where the attacker manipulates SQL queries to insert malicious code, which can lead to accessing sensitive information. Next, there is *cross-site scripting* (XSS). For this, an attacker will insert malicious scripts into a web page. This code might steal session tokens, deface websites, or redirect users to harmful sites.

- **Buffer overflow:** This happens when software writes large amounts of data to a buffer, which is temporary storage. This can overwrite nearby memory locations, allowing for the execution of code to crash an application.

- **Security misconfigurations:** This is where the attacker manipulates the configurations to gain access to sensitive information.

Because of this, you should do a rigorous security review of AI-generated code. You should also implement security features in the code, such as input validation as well as output sanitization, which will help prevent SQL injections.

Finally, some models may have inherent security flaws. This is especially the case with open-source models, which can be susceptible to *model poisoning*. This is where a hacker attacks it by manipulating the dataset and parameters. This can result in more hallucinations or even harmful output.

Black Box Concerns

LLMs are often referred to as *black boxes*. The reason is that their internal systems are not transparent. As a result, it is nearly impossible to explain how the AI comes up with its responses.

There are several reasons for this. First, LLMs are extremely large and complicated. It can be tough to understand how they work—even if there is access to the code and datasets.

Next, the developer of LLMs will often provide little detail about their models. A key reason for this is that they do not want their competitors to have proprietary information.

Interestingly enough, even open-source LLMs can be black boxes. How? The project may not include the weights and biases or the datasets. Only the source code is available.

However, transparency is certainly important. For businesses that are highly regulated, they need to understand how models work. This is often a requirement for compliance, but also to help engender trust with users.

To deal with these problems, there has emerged the field of *explainable AI* (XAI). This is about creating guidelines and tools—such as advanced AI models—to help make AI models more understandable.

Low-Quality Code

Sometimes an AI coding tool will create bloated code. A common reason for this is that the GenAI's underlying dataset for a particular task may be low quality. The system may also overengineer things. The result is that there could be unnecessary steps, too many functions, or redundant logic. There may also be inconsistent variable names. Besides, since GenAI does not understand software development, it will not have the ability to know about the overall architecture of the codebase.

No doubt, bloated code can be much harder to maintain and update. It can also make it challenging for systems that have low resources.

It's true that AI coding systems like GitHub Copilot have made progress in reducing the instances of bloated code. Yet it can still be an issue. To deal with it, you can use prompt engineering (covered in Chapter 5). You should also review your code and see where you can refactor it.

Limited Context Windows

An LLM has a *context window*. This is the number of tokens it can process.

For example, suppose you are using GitHub Copilot and have a chat session that has 10,000 tokens. But the context window is 5,000. This means that when the LLM processes the information, it will only use the last 5,000 tokens.

This can certainly be a big problem with software development. Codebases can have millions of tokens. So when an LLM is processing the information, it will not be able to get the whole context.

Context windows are getting larger. Yet this is not necessarily a solution either. One issue is the "lost in the middle effect." This is when a model essentially gets lost when processing the information in the midsection of the tokens.

Another issue is that context windows require substantial resources, which adds to the costs. They can also take longer to process.

Recency Problem

LLMs are trained on datasets up to a cutoff date. This is why the models are called *pretrained*. But this means there is a recency problem—that is, the responses are not up-to-date with the latest information. This can lead to problems like outdated frameworks and libraries, as well as deprecated features.

But some LLMs, like ChatGPT, can browse the web. This can help provide real-time information for the results. But there can still be problems because the model has not been trained on this information.

High Costs

The costs of building sophisticated GenAI systems are enormous. Dario Amodei, CEO and cofounder of Anthropic, has said that training a model could cost $5 billion to $10 billion for the years of 2025 to 2026.[13] Eventually, costs could soar to $100 billion.

Beyond training, there are also the huge costs for the datacenters, which need expensive *graphics processing units* (GPUs). These are chips that can process huge amounts of data in parallel. They are ideal for GenAI systems.

In 2025, Meta announced that it would spend $60 to $65 billion for datacenters and AI development.[14] As for Microsoft, it intends on spending $80 billion.

To get a sense of the scale of modern datacenters, consider what Meta CEO Mark Zuckerberg said on an earnings call[15]:

> "I announced last week that we expect to bring online almost a gigawatt of capacity this year. And we're building a two-gigawatt and potentially bigger AI datacenter that is so big that it will cover a significant part of Manhattan if we were placed there."

But with the costs soaring, may GenAI ultimately be nonviable? Will it be possible to create profitable businesses?

These are certainly big concerns. However, there are signs of innovation to bring more efficiency to GenAI.

An example of this is the launch of DeepSeek in early 2025. The founder, Liang Wenfeng, is a 40-year-old Chinese billionaire. He made his wealth by leveraging AI for his hedge fund.

But he saw an opportunity to disrupt the GenAI market. His team built an open-source model called R1, which showed comparable performance with leading LLMs from OpenAI and Anthropic. It also cost less than $6 million to train.[16]

Marc Andreessen, cofounder of Andreessen Horowitz, tweeted this[17]:

> "DeepSeek R1 is one of the most amazing and impressive breakthroughs I've ever seen—and as open-source, a profound gift to the world."

Responsible AI

In March 2016, Microsoft launched Tay on the Twitter platform. It was a sophisticated AI-powered chatbot. Unfortunately, it turned out to be a disaster. The chatbot would soon spew racist and sexist messages. Within 24 hours, Microsoft took down Tay and published a blog, which was an apology to its users.

As a large company, Microsoft understood that it could damage its brand and reputation if it failed to effectively deal with the risks of AI. It also knew that this would not be easy to do. AI technology can often have unintended consequences. It's also a quickly evolving technology and the potential threats can be murky. Then there are the tough issues with bias.

To help deal with these problems, Microsoft set forth a priority for *responsible AI* (this is also called ethical AI). This is about designing, developing, deploying, and monitoring

AI systems in a way that accounts for the technology's impact on society, the law, and ethical standards.

In 2019, Microsoft published its six principles of responsible AI:

- Fairness
- Reliability and safety
- Privacy and security
- Inclusiveness
- Transparency
- Accountability

This section takes a closer look at each of these.

Fairness

Fairness in an AI system is about treating people in a similar way. If there is a loan system, then the decision should be the same regardless of a person's race or gender.

Microsoft has the following recommendations for bolstering fairness:

- The AI team needs to understand how AI can jeopardize fairness.
- Members of the development team should have diverse backgrounds. This will allow for a better understanding of the potential impact of AI.
- There should be clear and actionable policies for fairness, such as to detect bias in datasets and algorithms.
- There should be ongoing human review of AI systems.
- Datasets need to reflect the real world.

Reliability and Safety

An AI system needs to be reliable and safe. It needs to adapt to unexpected situations. There should also be systems to ensure that the system is operating as intended, which involves extensive testing and monitoring.

This is what Microsoft advises:

- Create a list of unintended outcomes and edge cases.
- Implement an audit process for the AI.
- Document how the system operates.
- Understand the level of maturity of the AI system.
- Know when an AI system needs human intervention.
- Create strong feedback forms in the AI.

Privacy and Security

An AI system needs strong privacy and security protections. Often, AI systems use highly sensitive data. In fact, it's often this type of data that yields the best results, since it is highly personalized and relevant. This is why an AI system should make sure the training data is anonymous. Microsoft recommends that the data sent to the AI model be encrypted too.

There must also be a rigorous compliance program in place, which reflects all the compliance, regulatory, and legal requirements. But there should also be a focus on ethical AI considerations. All these are evolving as well, so the compliance program needs to be updated when necessary.

The AI application can have its own controls and guardrails. For example, there can be filters to evaluate if certain content is harmful before sending it to the user.

Inclusiveness

Inclusiveness for an AI system means that the AI system should benefit everyone. Here's how Microsoft explains it[18]:

> "For the 1 billion people with disabilities around the world, AI technologies can be a game-changer. AI can improve access to education, government services, employment, information, and a wide range of other opportunities. Intelligent solutions such as real-time speech-to-text transcription, visual recognition services, and predictive text functionality are already empowering those with hearing, visual, and other impairments."

For promoting inclusiveness, Microsoft has the following recommendations:

- Use the Inclusive Design toolkit. You can find it at `https://inclusive.microsoft.design/`.
- Test your AI system with people who have disabilities.
- Use accessibility standards.

Transparency

There must be transparency in an AI system. The developer of the model should provide an understandable description of how the features of the model impact the predictions. For example, if an AI system is for evaluating whether to lend money to a person, it should be clear how this is done.

If not, a system is vulnerable to bias, unintended outcomes, and privacy problems. However, a way to help mitigate these problems is to use simpler models, which are easier to understand and adjust.

Accountability

People who develop, run, and manage AI systems must be accountable for them. For this to be successful, there should be clear policies in place, which can be done by evaluating industry standards.

Something else that can help is setting up an internal review committee. They can help to set up the policies and enforce them. They can also be the source of ongoing feedback, as it's not uncommon for persons on an AI team to have concerns about certain projects.

Multimodel AI Coding

Another reason why it's important to understand how GenAI works is that AI coding systems are becoming *multimodel*. This means that they allow you to select different LLMs. For example, GitHub Copilot has this for Anthropic's Claude 3.5 Sonnet, Google's Gemini 1.5 Pro, and OpenAI's o1-preview. In the future, there will likely be more added to the platform.

So then how do you select a model? There is no right way. Evaluation is a combination of personal experience as well as the use of benchmarks. For example, when you are coding, you can experiment with several models and see which one works the best.

As for benchmarks for code generation, the following are common ones:

- SWE-bench: This is short for Software Engineering Benchmark. This includes a large dataset of GitHub issues, which are from 2,294 issue-pull request pairs from 12 popular Python repositories. These are used to test an LLM's ability to solve problems.

- HumanEval: OpenAI developed this dataset, which is based on 164 hand-crafted programming challenges. They all have a function signature, docstring, and body. The HumanEval test measures the ability of an LLM to generate and correct a function according to the docstring. These are evaluated based on several unit tests.

- EvoEval: This benchmark has 828 problems that span five categories, which are the following: difficult, creative, subtle, combine, and tool use. Then there are other types of problems, which are either verbose or concise. With these various dimensions, EvoEval has the benefit of providing a range of diverse use cases.

- BigCodeBench: Developed by Hugging Face, this has 1,140 hand-crafted tasks that involve function calls from 139 libraries and each has 5.6 test cases. The focus of BigCodeBench is to provide more complex instructions for the LLM.

- CodeScope: This has tests for 43 programming languages for eight different coding tasks. They are code summarization, code smell detection, code review, automated testing, program synthesis, code translation, code repair, and code optimization.

You can find these benchmarks on Hugging Face, which has leaderboards for the LLMs. But benchmarks will also be mentioned when an AI model developer launches a new model update. This may be from a blog post or research paper.

However, the benchmarks for LLMs have notable issues:

- **Slight changes in the prompts:** These can lead to major variations in the quality of results.

- **Memorization:** Since LLMs are based on large datasets, they may include information from the benchmarks. This is essentially like a student who cheats on an exam!

- **Practicality:** Some of the tests may be more theoretical and not real-world examples of what developers will encounter.

- **Edge cases:** A benchmark may focus mainly on common use cases. But when it comes to coding, the main challenges are often about understanding how to solve narrow issues.

- **Single solution:** Many of the benchmarks have only one solution. But software development usually has a variety of approaches.

- **Codebase context:** Benchmarks will focus on individual tasks or functions. But many of the real issues deal with the complexities of large codebases.

- **Frameworks:** These are critical for software development. But frameworks are often not part of the benchmarks.

How AI Makes Software Development Different

Traditional software development operates according to a fairly structured process. It starts with planning and putting together requirements. Then the developer breaks things down into functions. After this, there is the coding. However, there are certain tasks that are complex and require some research. This may mean checking out documentation for a framework or language or searching on Stack Overflow. Then there are unit tests, along with using a version control system like Git. Once the code is in good shape, there is the code review. Next comes the process to put the code into production.

This is fairly standard. But what happens when you use an AI coding system? There are some notable differences in the workflow.

First of all, the requirements process may be completed with the help of an LLM like ChatGPT or Claude. This can help to brainstorm ideas as well as to write the requirements document. The LLM will also provide suggestions for how to break down the code.

As for the coding process, you will likely be spending much of your time creating prompts with an AI coding system. This could be in the code editor, such as with autocompletion. You will also use a chat feature. This will create the code, along with an explanation. With a click, you can embed the code in your file.

When bugs pop up, you can use the AI coding system for this too. You simply put the error message in the chat box and you'll get an answer, along with suggested code.

The unit tests? An AI coding system will likely have a feature for this as well. And what about version control? Well, GitHub Copilot actually has a nifty tool for this. It uses GenAI to write descriptions for your pull requests.

An AI coding tool can also help with putting the code into production. It can provide suggestions on the scripts for the deployment, say on Azure or AWS.

Then there is documentation. You can have your AI coding system handle this too.

For the most part, when using this technology, you need to rethink your methods for software development. Often, when you approach a problem, you will think in terms of writing natural language prompts—not code. But doing this can be tricky. This is why it's important to understand the principles of prompt engineering.

All this can take some time to get comfortable with. This is especially true for those who have been programmers for many years. As with anything, habits can be tough to overcome.

Yet the benefits of using an AI coding system are clear—and worth making the changes. They help improve the speed and overall quality of your coding. You learn more about the benefits in the next chapter.

Types of AI Coding Tools

There are two main types of LLMs. There are those that are general purpose, such as ChatGPT, Gemini, and Claude. These LLMs can handle many tasks—seemingly almost anything. For example, they can help write a poem, plan a trip, or draw an image.

Next, there are specialized LLMs. As the name implies, these are focused on a category. This is where AI coding tools fit in. They just focus on software development. If you try to have the LLM do something else, you will often get a message that this is not possible. An AI coding tool is also usually part of an *integrated development environment (IDE)*. This is an application used to create, manage, and debug code, like VS Code.

As mentioned, you can use both general-purpose and specialized LLMs for software development. For example, you might want to create a logo for your application. In this case, you could use DALE-E for ChatGPT. Then you would use the AI coding system to see how to embed this in the code for your website.

There are many specialized AI coding tools available. This section looks at some of the most popular.

Amazon Q Developer

Amazon Q Developer can generate code for 25 programming languages, including Java, Python, and JavaScript. A key advantage of this tool is the integration with the AWS platform. You can use it to help with optimizing cloud costs, getting suggestions about which cloud resources to use, or correcting networking problems.

Amazon Q Developer is also effective in managing large enterprise projects. For this, it can handle complex porting of .NET from Windows and Linux. It can even manage mainframe modernization, Java upgrades, and VMware migrations.

Another benefit of Amazon Q Developer is its security features. It includes a code scanner, which can help detect threat vectors like log injections. It will even suggest remediations.

Finally, you can use Amazon Q Developer to build and manage AI, ML, and GenAI projects. You can use prompts for managing data pipelines and creating models.

Amazon Q Developer has a free tier that includes 50 interactions per month. The paid version costs $19 per month per user.

Gemini Code Assist

Gemini Code Assist works with more than 20 programming languages. It allows you to customize the system based on your private codebases, which means that you can get code suggestions that are more relevant.

Gemini Code Assist also works well with large-scale changes to a codebase. This includes updates to cross-file dependencies and version upgrades.

Of course, there are integrations with Google systems. Examples include Firebase, Colab, BigQuery, and Apigee.

The cost for Gemini Code Assist is $45 per month per user.

Cursor

Cursor has a grand vision "to build the engineer of the future: a human-AI programmer that's an order of magnitude more effective than any one programmer."[19]

True, this will likely take some time. But then again, Cursor has done a great job building a top-notch application.

A key has been its focus on innovation. Just look at its Composer feature. It allows for writing a prompt that can be applied to multiple files, which can greatly speed up development. It can also be effective for tasks like code refactoring or creating new components.

Cursor is one of the fastest growing GenAI companies. From April to October 2024, the annualized recurring revenue (ARR) soared from $4 million to $48 million.[20] In December 2024, the company announced that it raised $100 million at a $2.6 billion valuation.

The company offers two paid tiers for Cursor. The pro version is $20 per month per user and the business option is $40 per month per user.

V0

V0, which is developed by Vercel (a leading web hosting firm), is a web-based AI coding system. There is no extension for an IDE.

The main focus of V0 is to create user interfaces (UIs). For example, you can use a prompt to build a sign-up form, pricing page, or web page. V0 will then generate the code using React, Tailwind CSS, and Shadcn UI.

You can also upload an existing UI into V0 and it will generate the code for it. This can be a screenshot—say of a website you like—or a mockup you created. You can also upload a Figma design.

V0 has different pricing plans. There is a free tier, a premium version at $20 per month per user, and a team version at $30 per month per user.

Replit

Replit is a web-based IDE that supports more than 50 languages. Some of the nice benefits of this system include built-in source control and hosting capabilities. There are also helpful collaboration features.

As for AI coding, there is Replit Agent. When you create a prompt, this system will not only create the code but also set up the development environment, configuration, and dependencies. This greatly reduces manual tasks.

Replit Agent is available for the paid versions of Replit. One is Replit Core, which costs $15 per month per user. Replit Agent is also available for the Teams edition (but you have to reach out to the company for the pricing).

Summary

This chapter provided an overview of AI coding. You saw how this is a transformative development in programming that has involved a long history of abstraction.

The chapter then covered the basics of AI. This included topics like machine learning (ML) and deep learning (DL). Generative AI (GenAI) is at the heart of AI coding. It is based on training huge amounts of data and using the transformer model. However, AI coding has notable disadvantages. Some of the main ones are hallucinations, code quality, costs, and security.

Next, you learned about responsible AI. The chapter focused on Microsoft's six principles of responsible AI use: fairness, reliability and safety, privacy and security, inclusiveness, transparency, and accountability.

The chapter then explained how AI coding is different from traditional development and explored other tools available on the market (Amazon Q Developer, Gemini Code Assist, Cursor, V0, and Replit).

The next chapter covers GitHub Copilot versions, the setup of the software, and the core capabilities.

Exam Essentials

Understand the core concepts of GenAI and how they apply to AI coding.   GenAI is what creates the code, which is based on huge amounts of publicly available code from the Internet. The model does not know software development. Rather, the GenAI model essentially makes predictions based on the underlying data. Yet this often generates quality code. The probabilistic nature of GenAI tends to work well because programming languages are highly structured.

Understand that AI coding does not always generate quality code.   An AI coding system may generate hallucinations, which is code that is false or misleading. In many cases, this is not a problem, as the compiler often finds the problems, yet some may slip through. The AI-generated code may be functionally correct but generate results you do not want. In other cases, the code may even have security flaws. There are also times when the code is bloated. This is why it's important to always review AI-generated code before putting it into production.

Understand the risks of AI.   You need to understand how AI is vulnerable to problems with bias and security. You should also know about the principles of responsible AI, such as fairness, privacy, and transparency.

Understand multimodel AI coding.   For the exam, you need to know that AI coding systems allow you to use different LLMs. For example, GitHub Copilot has access to Anthropic's Claude 3.5 Sonnet, Google's Gemini 1.5 Pro, and OpenAI's o1-preview.

Review Questions

1. Which of the following best describes how AI coding systems impact software development?

    A. AI coding systems completely eliminate the need for programming knowledge.

    B. AI coding systems only generate syntax-correct code without logical errors.

    C. AI coding systems generate code but may introduce security vulnerabilities and inefficiencies.

    D. AI coding tools require no human intervention once deployed.

2. Which machine learning technique is used for training a model with labeled data?

    A. Reinforcement learning

    B. Supervised learning

    C. Unsupervised learning

    D. Deep learning

3. You are using GitHub Copilot and you want to select an AI model for the code generation. Which benchmark would be most relevant to evaluate its performance?

    A. SWE-bench

    B. ImageNet

    C. BERTScore

    D. Turing test

4. What is a key security risk when using code that's generated by AI?

    A. AI-generated code is always encrypted, making it hard to debug.

    B. AI-generated code may have threats like SQL injections and buffer overflows.

    C. AI-generated code usually has hardcoded passwords.

    D. AI-generated code is automatically reviewed for security threats.

5. You are building a recommendation system for an ecommerce platform. Which machine learning technique is best for this task?

    A. Supervised learning

    B. Reinforcement learning

    C. Unsupervised learning

    D. Deep learning

6. What is a common reason why AI-generated code may be difficult to maintain?

    A. It is always too cryptic to understand.

    B. It may be verbose, redundant, or inconsistent in variable naming.

    C. It follows detailed coding standards that are hard to modify.

    D. It is written in an entirely new programming language.

7. Which of the following is a major limitation of generative AI models like ChatGPT for software development?

    A. They cannot generate code for widely used programming languages.

    B. They only work for frontend development tasks.

    C. They may create hallucinations.

    D. They cannot generate code for frameworks.

8. Which of the following is an example of reinforcement learning?

    A. Training a chatbot using labeled data

    B. A model for a self-driving car that learns to navigate by receiving rewards for correct movements

    C. An AI model that uses unlabeled data for clustering

    D. A deep learning model that processes medical images for disease detection

9. What is one reason multimodel AI coding systems are becoming more popular?

    A. They allow users to select different AI models based on their requirements.

    B. They eliminate the need for debugging AI-generated code.

    C. They allow for supervised learning.

    D. They are trained exclusively on proprietary datasets.

10. Why is fine-tuning a large language model (LLM) more difficult than using retrieval augmented generation (RAG)?

    A. Fine-tuning requires specialized data science expertise.

    B. Fine-tuning is always less accurate than RAG.

    C. Fine-tuning does not allow customization of LLMs.

    D. Fine-tuning can only be done using open-source models.

11. A financial services company is using generative AI for its customer support system. What is a key risk if there is no human oversight?

    A. AI-generated responses will be too long.

    B. AI may generate misinformation.

    C. AI will be too expensive.

    D. AI eliminates the need for human customer support agents.

12. Why is it important to test an AI system for fairness before using it for hiring decisions?

    A. To ensure all candidates receive equal treatment regardless of demographics

    B. To increase the AI system's speed in processing applications

    C. To minimize the cost of hiring human recruiters

    D. To guarantee that the AI model replaces all human decision-making

13. A company is using AI to produce marketing copy. However, it is generating output that perpetuates stereotypes. What is the best approach to address this problem?

    A. Increase the model's training data size without modifying its content.

    B. Implement bias detection tools and adjust training data for diversity.

    C. Block all AI-generated content from being used in marketing.

    D. Reduce the AI's processing power to minimize bias.

14. Which of the following is a key responsibility of an AI ethics team within an organization?

    A. Ensuring that AI models always generate content at maximum speed

    B. Conducting periodic audits to identify ethical risks in AI models

    C. Developing AI tools without regulatory oversight

    D. Making AI the sole decision-maker in all business operations

15. A company wants to use AI-generated recommendations for its loan approvals. What should be a key concern when deploying this system?

    A. Ensuring the AI consistently approves high-dollar amount loans

    B. Making sure the AI model follows ethical and regulatory compliance guidelines

    C. Using the AI model to eliminate human oversight in loan approvals

    D. Optimizing the AI to increase the number of loans processed per day

16. Which of the following is a major privacy risk when using generative AI to process user data in a chatbot?

    A. AI models will automatically anonymize user data before processing it.

    B. AI-generated outputs may reveal sensitive user information.

    C. AI removes the need for data protection policies and compliance measures.

    D. AI models never store or process personal data.

17. Why are reliability and safety important in AI systems?

    A. AI systems must be able to adapt to unexpected situations and function as intended.

    B. AI should always replace human decision-making.

    C. AI does not require testing because it always produces accurate results.

    D. AI models are inherently safe and do not require monitoring.

18. How does inclusiveness improve AI systems?

    A. It speeds up AI response times.

    B. It allows AI to replace human interactions completely.

    C. It increases the AI's ability to make biased decisions.

    D. It ensures AI systems can serve diverse populations, such as people with disabilities.

19. Why is transparency a benefit for AI systems?

    A. It allows AI developers to keep their methods confidential.

    B. It ensures AI makes decisions without any human involvement.

    C. It helps users understand how AI makes decisions and detects potential biases.

    D. It removes the need for AI testing.

20. How can AI developers ensure accountability in AI systems?

    A. Rely solely on AI-generated reports to assess ethical concerns.

    B. Implement clear policies and industry standards.

    C. Allow only executives to review AI decisions without technical input.

    D. Assume that AI systems will naturally align with ethical standards over time.

Notes

1. *Financial Times* (August 2024). AI-Powered Coding Pulls in Almost $1bn of Funding to Claim "Killer App" Status. https://www.ft.com/content/4868bd38-613c-4fa9-ba9d-1ed8fa8a40c8 (accessed 26 February 2025).

2. https://x.com/paulg/status/1820887343307616684?s=43&t=cS1w1VZsy-iY3t91NeeUSw

3. *DistantJob* (December 2023). How Many Software Developers Are There in the World? https://distantjob.com/blog/how-many-developers-are-in-the-world/ (accessed 26 February 2025).

4. *Business Insider* (October 2024). Google CEO Says More Than a Quarter of the Company's New Code Is Created by AI. https://www.businessinsider.com/google-earnings-q3-2024-new-code-created-by-ai-2024-10 (accessed 26 February 2025).

5. GitHub Blog (February 2022). Introducing GitHub Copilot: Your AI Pair Programmer. https://github.blog/news-insights/product-news/introducing-github-copilot-ai-pair-programmer/ (accessed 26 February 2025).

6. https://x.com/karpathy/status/1608895189078380544?lang=en

7. https://x.com/karpathy/status/1617979122625712128?lang=en

8. Samuel, A.L. (1959) Some Studies in Machine Learning Using the Game of Checkers, IBM *Journal of Research and Development*, 3(3), pp. 210–229. https://doi.org/10.1147/rd.33.0210.

9. Arxiv (August 2023). Attention Is All You Need. https://arxiv.org/abs/1706.03762 (accessed 26 February 2025).

10. Future of Life Institute (March 2023). Pause Giant AI Experiments: An Open Letter. https://futureoflife.org/open-letter/pause-giant-ai-experiments (accessed 24 February 2025).

11. "Bias." Merriam-Webster.com. 2025. https://www.merriam-webster.com/dictionary/bias (accessed 25 February 2025).

12. Arxiv (May 2024). Bias Testing and Mitigation in LLM-based Code Generation. https://arxiv.org/abs/2309.14345 (accessed 26 February 2025).

13. *Business Insider* (April 2024). CEO of Anthropic—The AI Company Amazon Is Betting Billions on—Says It Could Cost $10 billion to Train AI in 2 Years. https://www.businessinsider.com/anthropic-ceo-cost-10-billion-train-ai-years-language-model-2024-4 (accessed 26 February 2025).

14. *The Wall Street Journal* (January 2025). Meta Spending to Soar on AI, Massive Data Center. https://www.wsj.com/tech/ai/meta-spending-ai-facebook-data-centers-9452a88f (accessed 26 February 2025).

15. *The Motley Fool* (January 2025). Meta Platforms (META) Q4 2024 Earnings Call Transcript. https://www.fool.com/earnings/call-transcripts/2025/01/29/meta-platforms-meta-q4-2024-earnings-call-transcri/ (accessed 26 February 2025).

16. CNBC.com (January 2025). NVIDIA calls China's DeepSeek R1 model "an excellent AI advancement." https://www.cnbc.com/2025/01/27/nvidia-calls-chinas-deepseek-r1-model-an-excellent-ai-advancement.html (accessed 26 February 2025).

17. https://x.com/pmarca/status/1882719769851474108

18. https://www.microsoft.com/cms/api/am/binary/RE4pKH5

19. Cursor Blog (January 2025). Series B and Automating Code. https://www.cursor.com/blog/series-b (accessed 26 February 2025).

20. *Techcrunch* (December 2024). In Just 4 Months, AI Coding Assistant Cursor Raised Another $100M at a $2.6B Valuation Led by Thrive, Sources Say. https://techcrunch.com/2024/12/19/in-just-4-months-ai-coding-assistant-cursor-raised-another-100m-at-a-2-5b-valuation-led-by-thrive-sources-say/ (accessed 26 February 2025).

Chapter

2

Introduction to GitHub Copilot

THE GITHUB COPILOT EXAM OBJECTIVES COVERED IN THIS CHAPTER INCLUDE, BUT ARE NOT LIMITED TO, THE FOLLOWING:

✔ **Domain 2: GitHub Copilot plans and features**

- Identify the different GitHub Copilot plans
  - Understand the differences between Copilot Individual, Copilot Business, Copilot Enterprise, and Copilot Business for non-GHE
  - Understand Copilot for non-GitHub customers
  - Define GitHub Copilot in the IDE
  - Define GitHub Copilot Chat in the IDE
  - Describe the different ways to trigger GitHub Copilot (chat, inline chat, suggestions, multiple suggestions, exception handling, CLI)
- Identify the main features with GitHub Copilot Chat
  - Identify the use cases where GitHub Copilot Chat is most effective
  - Explain how to improve performance for GitHub Copilot Chat
  - Identify the limitations of using GitHub Copilot Chat
  - Identify the available options for using code suggestions from GitHub Copilot Chat
  - Explain how to share feedback about GitHub Copilot Chat
  - Identify the common best practices for using GitHub Copilot Chat
  - Identify the available slash commands when using GitHub Copilot Chat

- Use GitHub Copilot in the CLI

  - Discuss the steps for installing GitHub Copilot in the CLI

  - Identify the common commands when using GitHub Copilot in the CLI

  - Identify the multiple settings you can configure within GitHub Copilot in the CLI

This chapter dives into GitHub Copilot, a software development tool powered by sophisticated generative AI. A developer interacts with GitHub Copilot using natural language, so as to create, debug, explain, and test code.

This chapter starts by looking at the many benefits of this powerful tool, like improved productivity and code quality. I back this up with a couple of case studies. Of course, the chapter also looks at the drawbacks. (Chapter 1 covered many of these, when it discussed the issues with LLMs.)

Next, this chapter explains the four versions of GitHub Copilot. It also looks at GitHub and the different editions of the service.

Then you get hands-on experience with GitHub Copilot by learning how to install it. The chapter also looks at many of its core features, including chat, slash commands, code completion, and Edits.

Finally, you will learn about the various integrations for GitHub Copilot, such as for GitHub.com, the GitHub mobile app, and the CLI (Command-Line Interface).

Benefits of GitHub Copilot

There are certainly many benefits to GitHub Copilot. It has become one of the most popular software tools. If anything, it's one of history's breakout applications.

One of the most important features of GitHub Copilot is that it provides real-time code suggestions based on the context. This can greatly increase productivity.

But there are other advantages. For example, the backing of Microsoft and GitHub have been critical for the success. GitHub Copilot can also help with full-stack development and with learning new languages.

In a way, GitHub Copilot is a *pair programmer*—always there to provide a helping hand.

Productivity

Developer productivity is an elusive concept. It's a combination of various factors, including efficiency, effectiveness, code quality, and speed.

Keep in mind that developer productivity has been a critical topic for decades. In the mid-1970s, Fred Brooks wrote a monumental book about the topic, entitled *The Mythical Man-Month*. In it, he set forth Brook's Law, which says: "Adding manpower to a late software project makes it later."

Having large teams often resulted in more complexities and communication problems. Projects would often be late and over budget.

In fact, Brook's Law is reminiscent of another axiom. It's from Amazon founder, Jeff Bezos. He came up with the "two-pizza rule." That is, a developer team should be no larger than what can be fed with two pizzas.

One of Brook's main contentions is that there was no magic formula for developer productivity. The fact is that software development usually takes time, involving preparation, clear requirements, collaboration, and code review. A lot can go wrong in the process.

It's true that there have been notable innovations that have helped developer productivity. Today's compilers are incredibly fast, with just-in-time (JIT) compilation, static analysis tools, real-time syntax completion, and autocompletion.

Another factor has been the proliferation of open-source projects. Frameworks like NextJS, React, and Vue.js streamline the process for creating sophisticated applications.

Then there are software development methodologies, such as Agile and Scrum. They are focused on having smaller teams, breaking down projects into simpler tasks, and developing on an incremental basis.

Even with all these efforts, the fact is that developer productivity has been challenging. Yet the emergence of AI coding systems has already shown that there can be major improvements.

Consider an extensive research study from GitHub.[1] It included feedback from more than 2,000 developers on their experience with GitHub Copilot. In terms of the measurement of productivity, it was based on a developer's ability to remain focused on a task, making steady progress and having a sense of satisfaction.

The results of the survey were standout. Around 60 to 75 percent of the developers said that they felt more fulfilled, less frustrated, and more focused on the tasks. A majority of the respondents also said that GitHub Copilot helped them stay in the flow of their work. Increased speed was another benefit, as 90 percent of the developers said that this tool helped them complete tasks faster. This was especially the case with repetitive tasks.

The research project also included a controlled experiment involving 95 developers. They were split into two groups—one that used GitHub Copilot and another that did not. For this, the developers had the task of building an HTTP server in JavaScript.

The results of the controlled experiment were striking. For those who used GitHub Copilot, they completed the task 55 percent faster on average. They also had a higher success rate, at 78 percent versus 70 percent.

GitHub has said that it plans to do even more research on developer productivity. Given the ongoing innovation with GitHub Copilot, it would not be surprising to see continued gains.

Code Quality

While GitHub Copilot will sometimes generate low-quality code, this appears not to be a serious problem. This is the conclusion of GitHub research.[2] The study involved over 200 seasoned developers. Each of them had the task of developing API endpoints for a web server. In terms of the evaluation of the coding, this included unit testing and expert reviews.

The results of the study were clear-cut. When using GitHub Copilot, 56 percent of the developers were more likely to pass all the unit tests. This was highlighted by a 13.6 percent increase in the average of error-free lines of code. This meant improved readability and reliability.

Pair Programming

Pair programming is a collaborative approach to software development. This is how it works. First, there is the "driver," who is the person who writes the code. Next, there is the "navigator." This person reviews the code as it is generated and provides feedback. This can involve helping with research or dealing with interruptions. With pair programming, it's common for the driver and navigator to switch roles. This helps improve engagement and share information.

There are different flavors of pair programming. One is called *mob programming* or *ensemble programming*. This is when there are three or more persons. Then there is *remote pair programming*. This became popular during the COVID-19 pandemic, when people did not go the office.

An academic study showed meaningful results for pair programming. It found develop-time cost improvements of 15 percent. This was due to improvements in design quality, better code reviews, and higher job satisfaction.[3]

In a way, GitHub Copilot acts as a virtual pair programming partner. It handles many of the same tasks that a navigator would. It can also do them near instantaneously. True, this is not to say that GitHub Copilot is a replacement for a pair programmer. There are many tasks that a human can do much better, especially those that involve creativity, innovation, and higher-order thinking.

Full-Stack Development

Full-stack development is about creating code for both the UI and on the server-side or backend of the application. Open-source frameworks have streamlined the process. Yet it can still be complicated. On the frontend, you need to understand JavaScript, HTML, and CSS. As for the backend, you need to understand server-side languages—like Java, Ruby or Python—as well as database management. Then there is the need for configuring the infrastructure, such as by using AWS, Azure, or Google Cloud.

But with GitHub Copilot, it's becoming easier to be a full-stack developer. It not only can handle the various languages, but even cloud deployment.

Granted, GitHub Copilot still has a ways to go. When building a full-blown application, there is still the need for much hand-crafted development. But more and more, GitHub Copilot is making the process much easier and automated.

Learning New Languages

Learning a new programming language can be challenging. Part of this is due to the need to change your mindset. After all, it's common to mix up concepts with a language you are already comfortable with. Moreover, programming languages will have their own quirks, which can take a while to learn. You'll also need to learn about the setup, the configuration, and the ecosystem, such as libraries. Then there are those programming languages that are fairly complicated. C++ comes to mind.

But with GitHub Copilot, the process of learning a new language is often much quicker and effective. It's like you have a smart teacher that you can ask questions—any time. When you do this, you not only get the code, but also an explanation. And if something is not clear, you can ask GitHub Copilot to provide a better explanation.

Even better, you can learn a language as you code. Take an example. Suppose you want to create a program that provides weather updates. You want to write this in Python. However, you do not know this language. Instead, you know how to develop in Java.

Here's a prompt:

I'm an experienced Java developer and do not know Python. But I want to write a program in Python that fetches current weather data from a free weather API. The program should display the temperature, humidity, and weather conditions for a given city. Could you write the code with detailed comments explaining what each line does?

GitHub Copilot will carry out the instructions. But suppose you have further questions. Here's another prompt:

I'm new to Python's indentation structure. Could you explain why we use indentation instead of curly braces to define code blocks?

You will go through this iteration process. So not only will you help build the program, but you'll also learn Python.

Attracting and Retaining Talent

Software is becoming a key competitive strength for many companies. Even nontechnology firms, such as Walmart, Liberty Mutual, and Nike, have large IT teams.

According to Microsoft CEO Satya Nadella:

> "I think a lot about what happens in computing. It is getting embedded in our world. Computing is a core part of every industry. A car is now a computer. Software skills are a valuable resource. I don't think in ten years we will have these demarcations. We won't have the tech industry and other industries."[4]

A big issue, though, is the global talent shortage for technical talent. This is predicted to reach 85 million people by 2030 and could result in the loss of $8.5 trillion in annual revenues.[5] Then there is the average turnover rate, which is 57.3 percent for software developers.[6]

GitHub Copilot can certainly address these issues. Of course many developers want to use advanced tools like GitHub Copilot to improve their work. A study reveals that 32 percent of these individuals have rejected a job opportunity because they did not like the tech stack they would work with.[7]

Besides, employers will want to use GitHub Copilot because it can allow for more effective software development. This is why it's common for employers to require—in job ads—that candidates have experience with this tool.

Microsoft and GitHub

In June 2018, Microsoft announced a deal to purchase GitHub for $7.5 billion. A key part of the deal was the synergy. The press release stated:[8]

> "Together, the two companies will empower developers to achieve more at every stage of the development lifecycle, accelerate enterprise use of GitHub, and bring Microsoft's developer tools and services to new audiences."

The vision was spot on. Consider that today GitHub is one of the fastest growing businesses within Microsoft. In 2024, the annual revenues were running at $2 billion, up from $1 billion in 2022.[9]

The biggest driver of the growth was GitHub Copilot. It accounted for more than 40 percent of the increase in revenues.

Then again, GitHub Copilot has become a must-have tool for more than 77,000 businesses across the globe. Just some include heavyweights like Honeywell, BMW, BBVA, AT&T, and FedEx.[10]

GitHub is one of the largest professional online networks as well. It boasts over 100 million users.[11] This has resulted in valuable network effects. This is where the value of a platform increases as more people use it. For GitHub, this has been through user feedback, getting the attention of potential partners, and attracting skilled employees—all helping to bolster innovation.

Case Studies

To better understand the benefits of GitHub Copilot, it can be helpful to look at a couple of case studies. They show the software in action. There is also the credibility of getting a first-hand validation of the software.

This section looks at case studies for AMD and SAP.

AMD

Founded in the late 1960s, Advanced Micro Devices (AMD) is a top semiconductor company. Its expertise is in developing cutting-edge chips for gaming systems, datacenters, AI, embedded systems, and PCs. But these systems often require sophisticated software. This is why the company has a large team of developers.

To help improve productivity and quality, AMD was an early adopter of GitHub Copilot. At first, there was skepticism among developers. Could AI really be effective when dealing with highly specific software systems?

Yet within a year of rolling out GitHub Copilot, the results went well beyond expectations. There were more than 5,000 developers who were using the software. An internal survey showed that the satisfaction rate was above 90 percent and that developers spent an average of two and a half hours per week with the tool.[12]

A key factor for the success was due to the ability of GitHub Copilot to tailor the AI model for AMD's stringent requirements for *firmware*. This is a specialized form of software that is integrated into devices. Usually, the code is stored in read-only memory (ROM) or flash.

But this means there is a need for high precision. Even one bug can be extremely costly, potentially costing millions in manufacturing. There can also be prolonged delays, which can hurt a company's revenues and allow competitors to get an edge.

With GitHub Copilot, AMD was able to use its own proprietary versions of firmware languages for Verilog and SystemVerilog. They allowed AMD to design chips based on its own architectures and electronic circuits.

The results of this approach were so impressive that some developers even transitioned from using the Vim editor to Visual Studio Code.

SAP

SAP is one of the world's largest software companies. Its software helps companies manage core business functions, such as finance, human resources (HR), supply chain, and procurement. As of early 2025, the company had more than 109,000 employees and over 100 development locations worldwide.[13]

When AI coding systems started to emerge, SAP saw that this technology could be transformative. The company set forth a comprehensive evaluation of various tools. Besides looking at productivity and speed of development, SAP also wanted a solution that could meet its rigorous legal and compliance requirements.

At first, the company launched a three-month pilot program, which included about 500 users. There was the collection of significant amount of data to determine the effectiveness of the software. There were also several developer surveys.

What was the conclusion? The results of the pilot were standout. Developers achieved a 25.6 percent code acceptance rate. This was for 9.3 million lines of code.

Moreover, with the time savings, the developers could focus more on higher valued-added tasks like improving product features and learning new skills. They could also devote more effort to code refactoring, documentation, and code reviews.

These helped deal with a common problem: *technical debt*. This is when software development is more about speed, not creating maintainable code. This can mean that the codebase becomes bloated and difficult to change.

In the end, SAP was impressed with the impact of GitHub Copilot. About 93 percent of the developers said that they found the tool easy to use and 79 percent felt it improved productivity. Within the first year of adoption, more than 18,000 developers wereon the system.[14]

Drawbacks of GitHub Copilot

Even with all its benefits, GitHub Copilot is not without its notable issues. In Chapter 1, you saw some of them. For example, sometimes GitHub Copilot hallucinates. Then there are the issues with code quality and security.

But there are also human-centered problems too. They include:

- Too much dependence on AI for coding
- Decline in programming and code review skills
- Lower motivation to explore new languages and technologies
- A decrease in human-based pair programming

But there are ways to deal with these problems. For example, developers should continue to build their software development skills. This should be a process that does not stop.

Next, there should always be a focus on determining where humans can be key. After all, GitHub Copilot is an assistant, not a replacement for software developers.

Versions of GitHub Copilot

The versions of GitHub Copilot include the following:

- Free Tier
- Copilot Individual
- Copilot Business
- Copilot Enterprise

There is much to choose from, and I cover the details of these tools in this chapter. I do this for those with non-GHE (GitHub Enterprise) environments.

You first get an overview of them. These versions are generally about different roles or organizations. For example, the Free Tier and Copilot Individual are mostly for solo developers, freelancers, students, and educators. While these are the most basic versions, they are still powerful. They include much of the core functionality of a modern AI coding system.

Next, Copilot Business and Copilot Enterprise editions are for larger organizations. There are numerous differences between the two. But one of the most important is that Copilot Enterprise provides more customization based on codebases and knowledge bases.

The different versions come with their own pricing arrangements. For GitHub Copilot Individual, the subscription is $10 per user per month or $100 per year. There is also a 30-day free trial, but you need to provide your payment method for this. You have the option to change the billing from monthly to annually and vice versa. You can also cancel at any time. This will take effect when the billing cycle is over.

If your subscription is upgraded to the Copilot Business or Enterprise edition, your Individual subscription will be automatically cancelled. You will receive a refund for the rest of the billing period.

As for Copilot Business, the subscription is set at $19 per user per month. Your organization will be charged at the end of each billing cycle for all the seats. For any new seats added during this period, the fee will be prorated according to the number of days remaining in the cycle. As for any seats removed, these will be accounted for at the beginning of the next billing cycle. A user will be able to use the service at the end of this period. This is the case so long as their access has not been removed.

Next, for the GitHub Copilot Enterprise system, the subscription is $39 per user per month. You can use your Microsoft Azure subscription for payment as well.

The Enterprise version allows you to create seats for Business users. The subscription for this is $19 per user per month.

Then what happens if you upgrade from the Business version to the Enterprise edition? For this situation, all the users will automatically be at the Enterprise level. You can also easily downgrade from Business to Enterprise.

To help encourage adoption, GitHub does provide some promotions. For example, some users can get free access to Copilot Individual. This is for the following:

▪ Students enrolled in a high school, secondary school, college, university, or homeschool. The minimum age is 13.

▪ Teachers, faculty members, and researchers. They must verify membership in an accredited educational institution.

▪ Maintainers of a popular open-source repository. GitHub has a verification process for this as well.

GitHub Accounts

To use GitHub Copilot, you need to have a GitHub account. GitHub is a platform to store, manage, and collaborate on code repositories. It also allows for issue tracking, pull requests, and code review tools. GitHub is built on *Git*, which is a popular open-source version control system.

There are three plans for GitHub: Free, Team, and Enterprise.

Free Plan

The Free plan comes with 2,000 CI/CD (Continuous Integration and Continuous Delivery) minutes/month. CI is when you often merge your code changes into a shared repository. This includes automated builds and tests. As for CD, this is the automation of the release process, in which the software is put into production. Essentially, with GitHub, you get the ability to automate these processes. You receive 500 MB of package storage for hosting—both public and private—for your software or dependencies on GitHub.com. It also includes features like these:

- **Unlimited public and private repositories:** You can host your projects using the web portal or through the CLI. Anyone can view public repositories on GitHub.com.

- **Automatic security and version updates:** GitHub will attempt to fix vulnerable dependencies. There will also be updates for older dependencies.

Team Plan

The Team plan comes with 3,000 free CI/CD minutes per month and 2 GB of package storage for public repositories. The cost is $4 per user per month. Here are other features:

- **Access to GitHub codespaces:** This is a web-based IDE, which has preconfigured containers and collaboration. It is very similar to VS Code. There is a fee for the compute resources used. It starts at $0.18 per hour. As for storage, it is $0.07 per GB per month.

- **Protected branches:** You can set up restrictions for merged code branches. This can be based on requiring reviews from selected collaborators or only permitting certain contributors to work on a specific branch.

- **Reviewers:** You can assign multiple users or a team to review a pull request.

- **Draft pull requests:** This makes it easy to discuss and collaborate on the pull requests before they are sent to formal review.

- **Code owners:** You can automatically request or require approval from selected contributors for changes to the code.

- **Required reviewers:** You can specify the number of approved reviews for pull requests before they are merged into a protected branch.

- **Pages and wikis:** With these, you can host your documentation. You can even host a basic website.

- **Environment deployment branches and secrets:** This means that a job cannot access secrets if they are defined in an environment. Rather, they need to run in a specific branch.

Enterprise Plan

The Enterprise version comes with 50,000 of CI/CD minutes per month for free public repositories. There is also 50 GB of storage for packages. The cost is $21 per user per month.

Some of the other features include:

- **Data residency:** This uses Microsoft Azure to select a region to deploy applications. This allows an organization to meet data residency requirements, such as in the European Union (EU).

- **Enterprise managed users:** You own and control the user accounts. This is done with your own identity provider.

- **Environmental protection rules:** A job will not start until all the environment rules are validated.

- **Repository rules:** You can place branch and tag restrictions across your organization.

- **Security:** Some of the features include Organization Controls (SOC) 1 Type 2, FedRAMP, SAML single sign-on, and advanced auditing.

When it comes to GitHub Copilot, the different versions available are based on the edition of GitHub you use. Copilot Free, Individual, and Business are for GitHub Free, GitHub Team, and GitHub Enterprise Cloud (this is the cloud deployment option for GitHub Enterprise). As for GitHub Copilot Enterprise, it's available for the GitHub Enterprise Cloud.

However, this does not mean an organization needs to host their code in GitHub repositories to use GitHub Copilot. You can use other platforms with this tool, such as GitLab or Bitbucket. But an organization still needs to have a GitHub account to manage its GitHub Copilot subscription.

GitHub Copilot Setup

As an individual user, the typical way to set up GitHub Copilot is to install one or two extensions for your IDE (integrated development environment), which are available for the following:

- JetBrains IDEs
- Vim/neovim
- Visual Studio
- Visual Studio Code (VS Code)
- Xcode

Among these IDEs, VS Code is the most updated in terms of integrating GitHub Copilot features. Others will likely be missing some of the features covered in this book. Because of this and the popularity of VS Code, it's the focus of the examples in this book. In fact, when using the free version of Copilot, you will need to use this IDE.

Exercise 2.1 explains how to install VS Code.

Installing the GitHub Copilot Extension on VS Code

1. Launch VS Code.

2. Select the Extensions icon on the left side of the screen.

3. A list of extensions will appear. On the top of this box, enter **Copilot** where it says Search Extensions in the Marketplace.

4. Click GitHub Copilot and then select the Install button. Do the same for GitHub Copilot Chat.

5. A popup will ask you to sign in to your GitHub account.

6. If GitHub Copilot is running, you will see the following icon on the top-right of the screen.

7. If you want to set up the extension for Copilot Business or Copilot Enterprise, you can request access. You do this by going to `https://github.com/settings/copilot` and selecting Get Copilot from an Organization.

Features of GitHub Copilot

Regardless of the version of GitHub Copilot, there are numerous core functions. They include chat, inline chat, code completion, and Edits. They allow you to do the common tasks of an AI coding system, like code generation, refactoring, debugging, and unit testing. But of course, there are the limitations, such as hallucinations, bias, and security, which I have already covered.

In terms of the best practices, one of the most important is to always review your code. You should also learn prompt engineering—such as by writing clear prompts—which is covered in Chapter 5. Then you should make sure you use security scans and frameworks.

The next sections look at the main components of this tool using VS Code.

Chat

GitHub Copilot Chat is essentially an AI-powered chatbot that is integrated with your code. Here are examples of the types of prompts you can use:

- *Add exception handling to the selected code.*

- *Generate a React custom hook that manages form state with validation, including email format, password strength, and matching password confirmation*

- *My Jest tests are failing with "Maximum call stack size exceeded." Review this recursive function and help me fix the stack overflow.*

- *Explain how this authentication middleware works. What security considerations should I be aware of?*

- *Convert this callback-based code to use async/await. Maintain error handling and ensure proper request cancellation.*

These just scratch the surface of what you can do with Chat. This section looks at the different approaches you can use for improving the performance of this powerful feature, such as with slash commands, @ references, extensions, and chat variables. But first, let's learn how to launch Chat, which is covered in Exercise 2.2.

If you are using the free version of GitHub Copilot, you are limited to 50 interactions per month for the Chat feature.

EXERCISE 2.2

Launching Chat

1. To activate Chat, click the GitHub Copilot icon at the top-right of the screen.

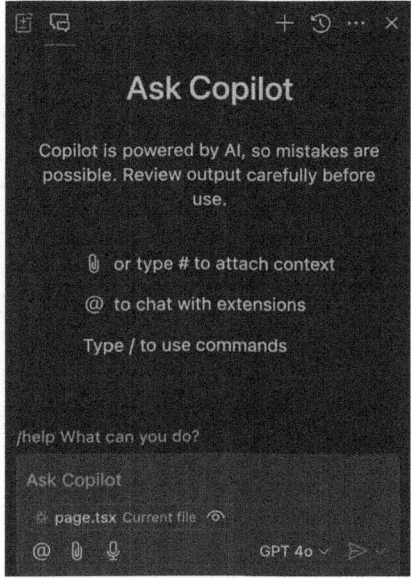

2. Where it says, Ask Copilot, you can enter your prompt.

3. When you are finished using Chat, you can click the X icon at the top of the screen.

By default, Chat is located on the right side of the IDE. If you want to move it, use your mouse to select the second icon from the top left and drag it.

With Chat, you enter your prompts at the bottom, which says Ask Copilot. Under this, you will see the name of the active file that is open in the IDE, which is `page.tsx`. In front of this is the icon for the React framework.

This is providing context for your prompts. For example, suppose you entered this: *Explain what this code does.*

GitHub will understand that you are referring to `page.tsx`. Figure 2.1 shows the response.

At the top, it says `>Used 1 reference`. If you click this, it shows that the response used `page.tsx`. Keep in mind that there can be multiple references for responses.

In Figure 2.1, the response provides a good explanation of the code. It first defines what it does and then breaks down the parts. Some words and phrases will have an icon of a

FIGURE 2.1   A response from GitHub Copilot.

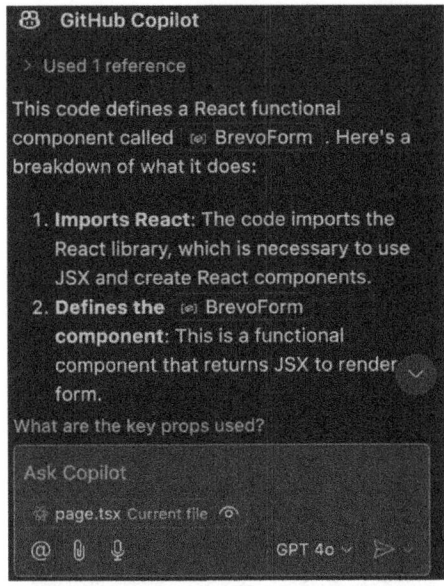

rectangle (in the figure, you can see this for BrevoForm). If you click this, it will take you to the part of the code that this refers to.

Sometimes you do not want to reference a file. This could be if you have a general question, such as "What is the Rust language?" You can disable the reference by clicking the eye-shaped icon at the end of the filename.

You can also add multiple files. For this, you will click the attach icon below the input box. Or you can drag a file from your IDE directory or desktop to the chat box.

You can also indicate the filename in your prompts. You do this by using the `#file` command. Here is an example:

#file:controller.py what does this do?

Below the input box, there are other useful commands:

- **Chat with Extension:** You use the @ reference to use a service or access your codebase. You'll learn more about this later in the chapter.

- **Voice (the microphone icon):** You can use your voice to create your prompts.

You can also select an LLM, which was covered in Chapter 1. Here are descriptions of each of the available models:

- **Anthropic's Claude 3.5 Sonnet:** This has become a popular model for software developers. Then again, *Claude 3.5 Sonnet* has shown high levels of performance for code generation, bug fixes, maintenance, and optimization. It can also engage in complex, multi-step coding tasks and refactoring. Based on Anthropic's metrics, Claude 3.5 Sonnet solved 64 percent of the evaluation problems. This compared to 38 percent for the prior model, which was Claude 3 Opus.[15]

- **Google's Gemini 1.5 Pro:** A key feature is the context window, which processes up to two million tokens. This translates into roughly 160,000 lines of code. As for the benchmarks, *Gemini 1.5 Prof* does quite well, scoring 71.9 percent on HumanEval and 77.7 percent on Natural2Code.[16]

- **OpenAI's o1-preview and o1-min:** The *o1 preview* model has shown strong performance with reasoning, including complex code constraints and edge cases. This helps improve the code quality and reliability. *o1-mini*, on the other hand, is a less powerful model. But it is also quicker and 80 percent less expensive. And the coding capabilities are still fairly strong.

Other Chat Features

At the top of the Chat interface, you'll see several icons:

- **Copilot Edits:** This allows you to perform code modifications across multiple files. We'll look at this in more detail later in this chapter.

- **New Chat (+):** This will create a new chat session. It's a useful feature because of how the context window works. In some cases, you do not want the chat session to be a part of your prompt. This could actually provide less effective responses. But by creating a new chat, you will start with a blank slate.

- **Show Chats:** This will show your prior interactions for each chat session. After all, sometimes you might want to see a prior response. By using Show Chats, you will click on the thread.

- **More (…):** Clicking this, you'll get a drop-down for several options. You can open Chat in the IDE's editor or as a new window. You can also see a list of new features, which will show up in your editor. Finally, there is the option to send user feedback to GitHub.

Slash Commands

A slash command—which is represented with the / character—is essentially a way to shorthand your prompts. This is an example: */explain*. With this, GitHub Copilot will identity your cursor in the IDE's editor or select code, and then write an explanation.

You can also add details for a slash command. Consider this:

/explain the Car class and its methods

This can be useful since the response will not have extraneous details.

There are many slash commands available. Let's take a look:

- */fix* provides fixes for issues with your code.

- */clear* creates a new chat session.

- */test* generates unit tests.

FIGURE 2.2   Suggested code scaffold for a Node.js project.

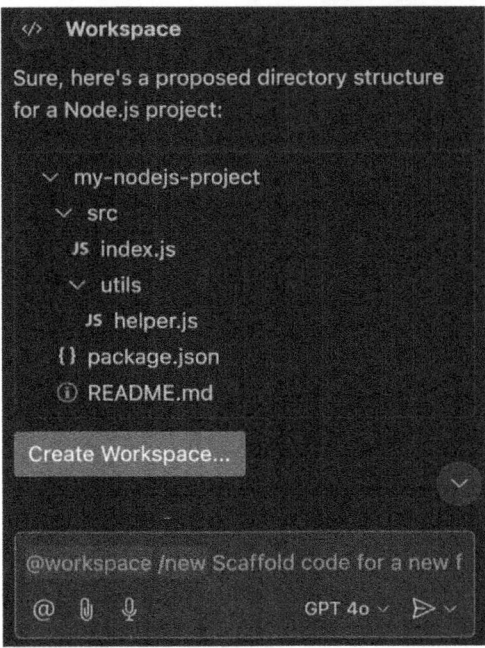

- *setupTests* creates the files to set up Playwright in your project. This is an open-source framework—created by Microsoft—that is for end-to-end testing of web applications.

- */fixTestFailure* provides suggestions for fixes when a unit test fails.

- */newNotebook* creates a new Jupyter notebook. This can be used for data science projects in your IDE.

- *startDebugging* generates a launch configuration, which you can use for debugging in VS Code.

- */Search* suggests query parameters for workspace search in VS Code.

- */new* sets up the files for the scaffolding of a new project. An example prompt is */new node.js project*. GitHub Copilot will show the files and you'll click Create Workspace to generate this in your IDE. You can see this in Figure 2.2.

@ References

GitHub Copilot has numerous built-in @ references. You will often use these along with slash commands for your prompts.

The following sections look at *@workspace, @terminal*, and *@vscode*. After that, you will learn how these are used for extensions.

@workspace

@workspace refers to your project's code workspace. It will attempt to understand the structure, such as the relationships with the different parts of the code or design patterns.

However, *@workspace* may not cover everything because of the context window of the LLM. Generally, it will evaluate the following:

- The file system structure of your project.
- The relevant parts of your code. This will focus on classes, methods, and comments.

Note that *@workspace* does not have access to your Git history.

Here are some sample prompts:

- *@workspace find the calculateTotal function*
- *@workspace /new Python Flask application that has Jinja2 templates*
- *@workspace what are the improvements for the data processing module?*
- *@workspace any hardcoded credentials?*

Sometimes, Copilot will assume that you want to use *@workspace*. This is common when you are doing a search. The LLM will automatically include *@workspace* in the prompt.

@terminal

With *@terminal*, you can reference your IDE's shell. You can use this to ask questions about commands or for debugging.

Here are some sample prompts:

- *@terminal /fix*
- *@terminal find the largest files in the src directory*
- *@terminal how to update an npm package*

@vscode

@vscode allows you to ask questions about VS Code, such as its features and settings.

Here are some sample prompts:

- *@vscode How do I change the color theme?*
- *@vscode How can I debug a Node.js application?*
- *@vscode How do I customize keyboard shortcuts?*

Extensions

In May 2024, GitHub announced the GitHub Copilot Extensions program. This allows third parties to create extensions for their own platforms and make them available to Chat.

Extensions are available for all Copilot versions. In terms of the benefits, one of the most important is that there is no switching in the IDE. This allows developers to stay in the flow. Next, extensions essentially allow for more customization.

To use a GitHub Copilot extension, go to the GitHub Marketplace at `https://github.com/marketplace?type=apps&copilot_app=true`. On the left side of the screen, select Copilot and you will see a list of the extensions. You can see this in Figure 2.3.

Here are some of the extensions:

- **DataStax:** This integrates with the Astra DB, which is a serverless database. You can use Chat to create queries and code for it.

- **JFrog GitHub Copilot Extension:** This is an integration with the JFrog platform, which is an open-source package management and knowledge system.

- **Neon Database:** You can chat with your neon documentation, which includes the context from your repository.

Using an extension is fairly straightforward. You will use an @ reference for it. For example, with the JFrog extension, these are sample prompts:

- *@jfrog Suggest some secure npm packages for handling HTTP requests*

- *@jfrog Are there any known vulnerabilities in the latest version of lodash?*

- *@jfrog Are we currently using any versions of Apache Kafka in our projects?*

- *@jfrog Is it permissible to use Express.js 4.17.1 under our company's open-source usage policies?*

You can also build your own extension. This can be for the Marketplace or for internal purposes.

FIGURE 2.3   The GitHub Marketplace.

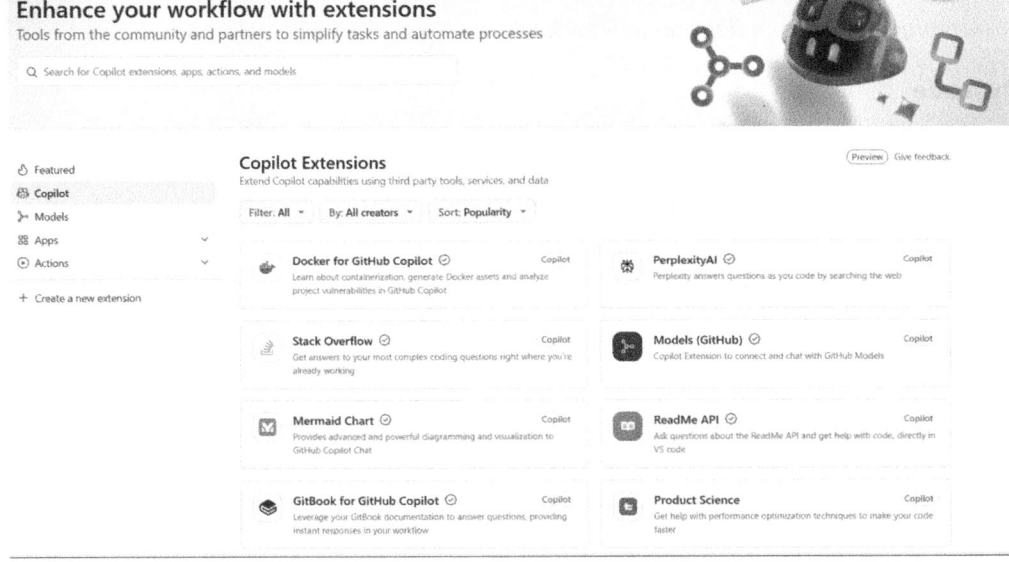

GitHub provides a toolkit for building extensions. It has a CLI for debugging, SDKs (software development kits), and sample code. You can find more information about these resources at `https://docs.github.com/en/copilot/` `building-copilot-extensions/about-building-copilot-extensions`.

Chat Variables

Earlier in the chapter, you saw how to use the `#file` command. This is actually called a *chat variable,* and there are various available. They help improve the results of GitHub Copilot by adding more context to your prompts.

Here are the other chat variables:

- *#editor* is the context for the code in the active file in the IDE's editor. Example prompt: *Review the code in #editor and suggest improvements.*

- *#selection* provides the context for the code selected in the editor. Example prompt: *Optimize the performance of the #selection.*

- *#terminalLastCommand* is the context for the terminal's last command that has been executed. Example prompt: *Explain #terminalLastCommand.*

- *#terminalSelection* is for the context for the active terminal's selection. Example prompt: *Analyze the output for #terminalSelection.*

Inline Chat

Inline chat allows you to use GitHub Copilot Chat in your IDE. It's a convenient feature since it is seamless with your coding experience.

Exercise 2.3 outlines the steps for using inline chat.

EXERCISE 2.3

Using Inline Chat for GitHub Copilot

1. Highlight this code in the IDE.

```
1  def find_max_value(numbers):
2      max_val = numbers[0]
3      for num in numbers:
4          if num > max_val:
5              max_val = num
6      return max_val
7
8  numbers = [3, 7, 2, 9, 5]
9  print(find_max_value(numbers))
```

2. Right-click your mouse and select Copilot. Then click Editor Inline Chat. There is also a short code for this. It's Ctrl+I for Windows and ⌘+I for the Mac. After this, you will get the inline chat interface above the code.

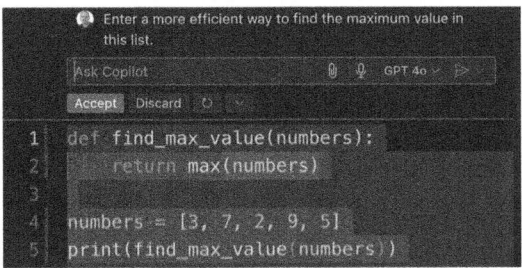

3. Enter this prompt: **Enter a more efficient way to find the maximum value in this list.**

4. This is what you will see.

5. It's a much more efficient code block. You can either accept or discard it. There is also an icon that will rerun the prompt.

Inline chat has limited options, though. You can add files, use voice prompts, and select an LLM. There are also limitations on the shorthand you can use. For example, the slash commands available are for */explain, /fix, /explain*, and */doc* (this is to set docstrings).

Code Completion

Code completion is like autocomplete—but it uses an LLM to generate suggested code. This is based on the context of the code you are creating.

Let's say you are developing a program to calculate factorials. You will write the following in VS Code:

```
def factorial(n):
```

The LLM will understand that you are creating a function in Python and that it is likely for a factorial. Figure 2.4 shows the response.

FIGURE 2.4   Code completion in GitHub Copilot.

There is AI-generated code for the factorial function. This is in gray, which is known as ghost text. You can accept this code by pressing the Tab key. Or, if you do not want to use it, you can press the Escape key.

This example shows the importance of using descriptive functions, methods, and variables. If you do not, you will not get good results.

There is another approach for autocompletion. You can use a comment in your IDE and follow this up with a prompt:

 # Function to calculate the factorial of a number

You will get the ghost text for the function.

Note that if you have the free version of GitHub Copilot, you are limited to 2,000 code completions per month.

Edits

The Edits feature in GitHub Copilot allows you to use AI across multiple files in your workspace. While this is not mentioned as a topic in the GitHub certification study guide, it seems likely it will appear on future exams. Edits is something GitHub has been promoting. In fact, it would not be surprising if it ultimately replaces Chat.

There are different ways to access Edits:

- **Keyboard Shortcut:** For Windows, it's Ctrl+Shift+I and for the Mac, it's ⇧⌘ (Shift+Command+I).

- **Copilot icon:** Click this at the top-right of your IDE. In the drop-down, there will be an option for Edits.

- **Chat:** When you're in the Chat interface, you can click the top-left icon.

Figure 2.5 shows the Edits feature.

Above the input box, there is "Working Set." This shows the files you want Edits to work on. Currently, the limit is 10.

There are different ways to add a file:

- **Add Files Option:** Click Add Files or use the shortcut (Ctrl+/ for Windows and Command+/ for Mac). This will show a list of recently used files in your workspace and you can click the one you want. You can also use the search box to find files.

FIGURE 2.5   Edits feature in GitHub Copilot.

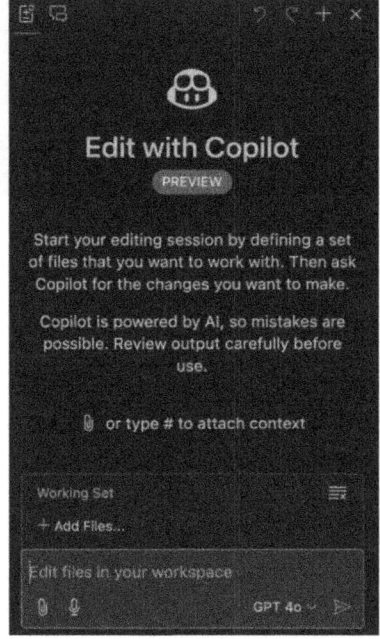

- **Drag and Drop:** You can select and drag files from your IDE or your desktop. You can also do this for folders.
- **Context Menu:** You can right-click a file from your IDE, click Copilot, and then select Add File to Copilot Edits.

But you do not necessarily have to add files. If you do not, Edits will assume that you want the changes made to the workspace.

Say you want to do this for a to-do app you are creating. You will enter this prompt:

Add a feature to mark tasks as completed.

Create a filter to show only overdue tasks.

Furthermore, when crafting the prompts for Edits, it's important to be clear and detailed about the changes you want to implement. For more complex tasks, it's a good idea to break them down into smaller steps.

Figure 2.6 shows the response.

In the file area, you can see that Edits has determined which ones to include. Above this, there are brief descriptions of the changes for each file.

In the middle of your IDE, Edits will navigate to each of the proposed changes. At the bottom, there is a menu that allows you to accept or discard them. You can also cycle through the others with the up or down arrows.

FIGURE 2.6   Response from Edits.

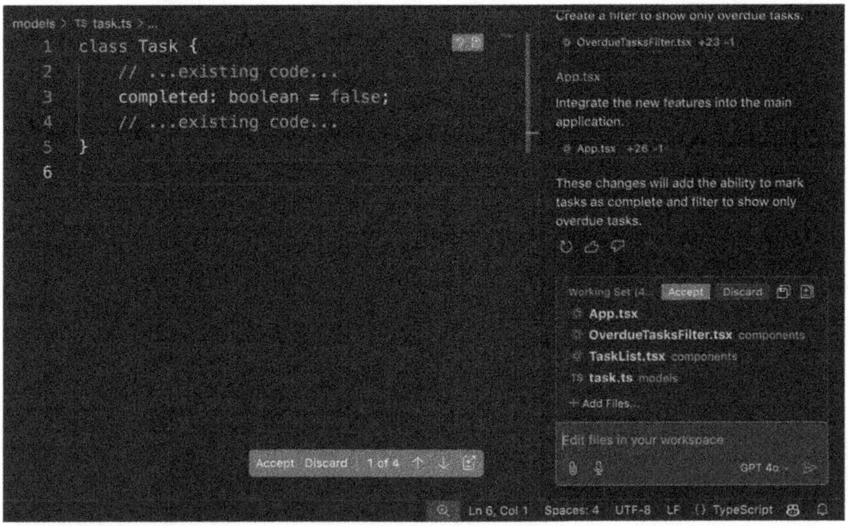

For this process, you need to be wary. Make sure you evaluate what these changes will mean for your application.

Of course, you can also continue improving your project by using more prompts.

Integrations

To use GitHub Copilot, you are not limited to an IDE. GitHub has been actively embedding the technology across various platforms. These include GitHub.com, GitHub Mobile, Azure, and the CLI for your IDE.

GitHub.com

The four versions of Copilot are integrated into GitHub.com. This is definitely a convenient feature, as many developers spend much time working with repositories. This can also help improve collaboration with your team.

To use GitHub Copilot, you will log in to GitHub.com and then click the Copilot icon on the top right of the screen. It will ask you to select a repository. Then you will get access to the Chat interface, which you can see in Figure 2.7.

If you click ... at the top right, you will get a few options, such as to delete a conversion, view all conversations, and give feedback. Next to this is a button that will expand the interface for the whole screen.

In the middle of the screen, You will get the response from Copilot, as well as suggested prompts. As for the input box, you can use it to ask questions about your repositories. Below this, you can add files or extensions.

FIGURE 2.7   GitHub Copilot Chat interface in GitHub.com.

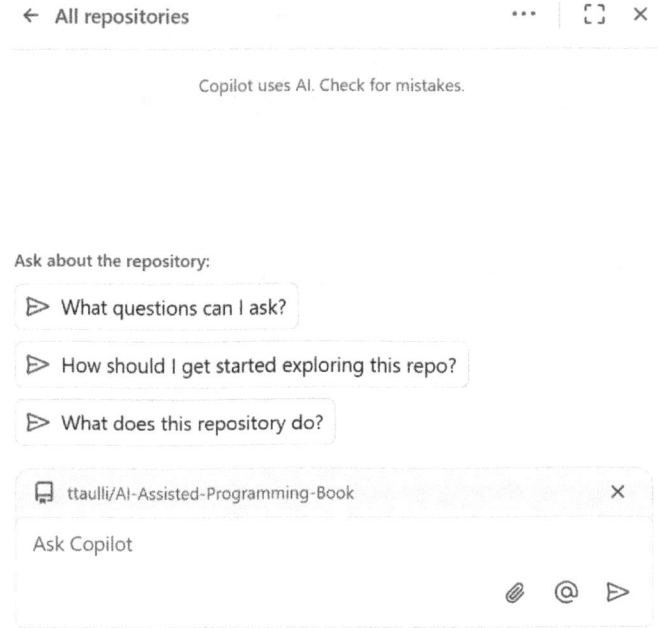

Here are some other useful features:

▪ **Pull Request Summaries:** This uses an LLM to generate summaries based on the context of your repository. This feature is particularly useful, as about 40 percent of pull requests lack descriptions.

▪ **GitHub Action Jobs:** Whenever there is a failure with these, there can be considerable disruption. GitHub Copilot will provide analysis to help identify the problems and suggest fixes.

GitHub Mobile

GitHub Copilot Chat is available on the GitHub mobile app, which is on iOS and Android. If you have the free or Individual versions, then the access is automatic. However, if you're using GitHub Copilot Business or Enterprise through your organization, you need your administrator to enable GitHub Copilot Chat.

Note that with GitHub Copilot Enterprise, developers can connect Copilot to their organization's private repositories.

GitHub Copilot for Azure

GitHub Copilot for Azure is an extension that integrates with GitHub Copilot Chat in Visual Studio Code. With this, you can manage Azure services within the code editor. This is done by using the *@azure* command.

Here are some of the features:

- **Learn about Azure:** Developers can ask questions about Azure services, getting detailed and up-to-date responses.
- **Resource Management:** You can get summaries about your Azure account, such as for resource usage.
- **Troubleshooting:** The *@azure* command is helpful in detecting problems and suggesting fixes. This is done by analyzing the logs.
- **Cost management:** You can get estimates on Azure costs.

GitHub Copilot in the CLI

With GitHub Copilot in the CLI, you can get explanations and suggestions for commands for your terminal. However, this feature is not available in the free version of Copilot.

Exercise 2.4 shows the steps to set up the CLI.

EXERCISE 2.4

Setting Up GitHub Copilot in the CLI

1. You need to install the GitHub CLI in your terminal. For the Mac, you can use Homebrew, MacPorts, Conda, Spack, or Webi. For example, if you have Homebrew, you use this command: `brew install gh` (depending on the security of your Mac, you may have to precede this with the `sudo` command). As for Windows, you can use WinGet, scoop, Chocolately, Conda, or Webi. So, if you have WinGet, the command is `winget install --id GitHub.cli`.

2. Issue the `gh auto login` command. Go through the authentication process to connect to your GitHub account.

3. Install the Copilot CLI extension with `gh extension install github/gh-copilot`.

4. Verify the installation with `gh copilot -help`. If you see the help information, then the installation was successful.

5. The extension will periodically be updated. To upgrade the software, use the `gh extension upgrade gh-copilot` command.

As for using Copilot in your CLI, you have a few commands to work with. For example, with the `gh copilot explain` command, you can get help with CLI commands. It could be something like:

```
gh copilot explain "chmod -R 755 /var/www"
```

FIGURE 2.8   Response from the GitHub Copilot in the CLI.

```
Welcome to GitHub Copilot in the CLI!
version 1.0.5 (2024-09-12)

I'm powered by AI, so surprises and mistakes are possible. Make sure to verify any ge
nerated code or suggestions, and share feedback so that we can learn and improve. For
 more information, see https://gh.io/gh-copilot-transparency

Explanation:

  • chmod is used to change the permissions of files and directories.
    • -R specifies that the permission changes should be applied recursively
    to all files and directories within /var/www.
  • 755 is the permission mode being set.
      • 7 sets read, write, and execute permissions for the owner.
      • 5 sets read and execute permissions for the group.
      • 5 sets read and execute permissions for others.
  • /var/www is the directory where the permission changes are being
    applied.
```

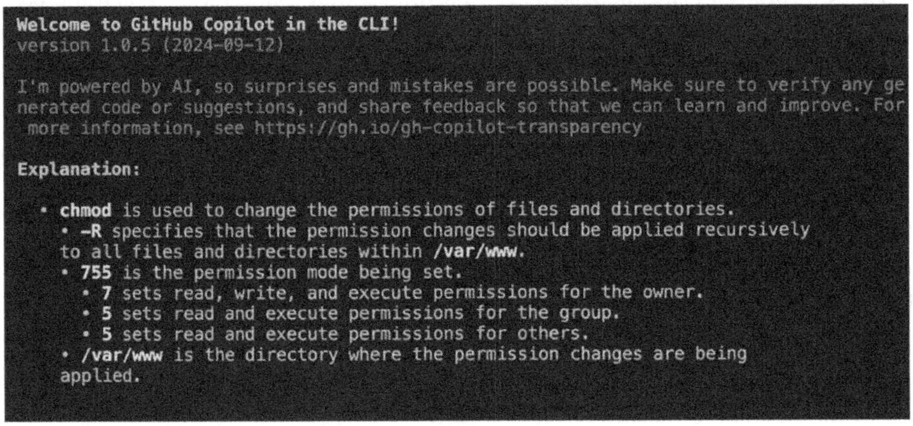

Figure 2.8 shows the response.

If you want GitHub Copilot to suggest a command, you can use gh suggest:

```
gh copilot suggest "List all running Docker containers"
```

Copilot will ask you for the type of command you are looking for, with the following options: generic shell command, gh command, or git command. Select the first one. Then you will select Explain command and GitHub Copilot will suggest docker ps.

Next, you can configure the CLI. For example, you can use aliases for the commands, which can help streamline the process. Suppose you often use this command: gh copilot suggest. For it, you can set an alias of gcs (or whatever you want).

You will need to change the confirmation settings. This what you do when using bash or zsh:

```
echo 'alias gcs="gh copilot suggest"' >> ~/.bashrc
source ~/.bashrc
```

Or you can use this for PowerShell:

```
echo 'alias gcs="gh copilot suggest"' >> ~/.bashrc
source ~/.bashrc
```

When you run a command suggested by the CLI, you will get a prompt to confirm it. You can change this in the confirmation settings by running gh copilot config. Then select Default Value for Confirming Command Execution, and select the default setting you want.

Summary

This chapter covered the benefits of GitHub Copilot. Just some of them were improved productivity and code quality. You looked at two case studies that emphasized these benefits, AMD and SAP. You then looked at the drawbacks of GitHub Copilot. These include too much dependence on AI coding, a decline in code review skills, lower motivation to explore new languages, and a decrease in human-based pair programming. After this, you learned about the four versions of GitHub Copilot, as well as the GitHub platform. Then you went through the installation process.

Next, you looked at the core capabilities of the different versions. They include features like chat, slash commands, code completion, and Edits. The chapter ended by covering the various integrations with GitHub Copilot, like for GitHub.com, the GitHub mobile app, and the CLI.

The next chapter reviews the differences among the four versions of GitHub Copilot.

Exam Essentials

Understand the four plans of GitHub Copilot.   You should know about the core features. Some of them include chat, code completion, and inline chat. It's also a good idea to learn about GitHub Copilot Edits, which is becoming increasingly important. Then you should review the different versions of the GitHub service and why this is required for using GitHub Copilot.

Know how the Chat feature works.   This includes many capabilities. You should understand how to activate Chat. You also need to know some of its key functions. These include slash commands and @ references. They allow for enhancing the prompts. You should also know how to attach files, which add context for the LLM.

Learn about the CLI.   You should know about how to install the CLI for GitHub Copilot. This is integrated in the GitHub CLI. It allows you to understand the numerous commands and to get recommendations for different scenarios. Finally, you should know about how you can configure the CLI.

Review Questions

1. What is a key advantage for developers when using GitHub Copilot?

    A. It replaces the need for manual testing of code.

    B. It automatically refactors all code without developer input.

    C. It provides real-time code suggestions based on the context.

    D. It eliminates the need for version control systems.

2. How does GitHub Copilot improve developer productivity?

    A. By replacing the need for manual testing of code.

    B. By reducing the time spent on repetitive coding tasks.

    C. By enforcing a fixed coding style for all projects.

    D. By automating software deployment to production servers.

3. Which GitHub Copilot plan is best for large organizations that require strong security and compliance capabilities?

    A. GitHub Copilot Free

    B. GitHub Copilot Individual

    C. GitHub Copilot Business

    D. GitHub Copilot Enterprise

4. What is the role of GitHub Copilot Chat in the development process?

    A. It automates deployment pipelines for cloud-based applications.

    B. It provides interactive, context-aware assistance within the IDE.

    C. It replaces the need for human developers in software projects.

    D. It automatically merges pull requests without review.

5. Which of the following is a correct way to activate GitHub Copilot's inline suggestions?

    A. Using specialized GitHub Job Actions

    B. Typing a comment or starting a code snippet

    C. Opening the Copilot CLI tool

    D. Manually exporting the code to Copilot Chat

6. What is one reason GitHub Copilot helps with full-stack development?

    A. It generates UI and backend code across multiple programming languages.

    B. It eliminates the need to manually configure core cloud infrastructure.

    C. It fully automates all aspects of frontend and backend development.

    D. It ensures all generated code is free from security vulnerabilities.

7. How does GitHub Copilot help developers with learning a new programming language?

    A. By automatically translating Java code into Python and vice versa

    B. By providing code completions with explanations when developers prompt for help

    C. By enforcing strict rules to prevent syntax errors

    D. By preventing developers from using old programming methods

8. What is one common disadvantage of using GitHub Copilot?

    A. It does not have third-party integrations.

    B. It requires developers to use only Microsoft Visual Studio Code.

    C. It produces code that requires manual validation for accuracy and security.

    D. It replaces the need for human developers in software engineering.

9. A developer wants to use GitHub Copilot in the command line. What must they do first?

    A. Install the GitHub CLI and authenticate their account.

    B. Disable GitHub Copilot in the IDE.

    C. Manually download the Copilot AI model for offline use.

    D. Configure GitHub Copilot to run only on private repositories.

10. Which of the following is a way to improve GitHub Copilot Chat performance?

    A. Limiting interactions to only 10 per day

    B. Using clear prompts

    C. Avoiding the use of slash commands

    D. Using only single-word prompts

11. A developer wants GitHub Copilot to generate test cases for their code. Which feature should they use?

    A. GitHub Actions

    B. The */test* slash command in Copilot Chat

    C. The `.copilotignore` file

    D. The GitHub Enterprise API

12. What is the role of slash commands in GitHub Copilot Chat?

    A. They provide a shorthand way to trigger specific AI responses.

    B. They allow Copilot to edit GitHub repository settings.

    C. They enable direct communication with GitHub support.

    D. They disable Copilot's AI suggestions.

13. A developer wants to set up GitHub Copilot in Visual Studio Code. What is the first step?

    A. Manually downloading the AI model

    B. Installing the GitHub Copilot extension from the VS Code Marketplace

    C. Disabling version control integration

    D. Configuring `.copilotignore` before installation

14. What is one major limitation of GitHub Copilot?

    A. It only works with Microsoft programming languages.

    B. It may generate code that contains security vulnerabilities.

    C. It prevents developers from using external libraries.

    D. It requires all projects to be public.

15. Which action can improve GitHub Copilot's performance when generating code suggestions?

    A. Using precise and well-structured comments in the code

    B. Limiting GitHub Copilot to only one programming language

    C. Running the AI model in offline mode

    D. Disabling the inline suggestion feature

16. Which command allows developers to use GitHub Copilot in the CLI?

    A. `copilot start`

    B. `gh copilot chat`

    C. `copilot run`

    D. `git enable-copilot`

17. A developer wants GitHub Copilot to explain an error message in the terminal. Which command should they use?

    A. `gh copilot explain "error message"`

    B. `git error --fix`

    C. `copilot debug --show-details`

    D. `cli copilot read-error`

18. What is a key advantage of using GitHub Copilot's inline chat feature?

    A. It allows developers to get AI-generated suggestions without leaving their code editor.

    B. It automatically merges pull requests based on AI analysis.

    C. It eliminates the need for manual debugging.

    D. It enables AI-driven deployment automation.

19. What is a key advantage of using GitHub Copilot's Edits feature?

   A. It disables manual code editing.

   B. It generates AI-driven deployment strategies.

   C. It automatically resolves merge conflicts.

   D. It allows developers to modify multiple files simultaneously.

20. A developer is working on a project and wants GitHub Copilot to suggest improvements to a function. What is a way to accomplish this?

   A. Use the */explain* slash command and manually review the function.

   B. Delete the function and rewrite it from scratch.

   C. Disable Copilot's suggestions and work without AI assistance.

   D. Use the */deploy* slash command to optimize the function.

Notes

1. GitHub Copilot Blog (September 2022). Research: Quantifying GitHub Copilot's Impact on Developer Productivity and Happiness. https://github.blog/news-insights/research/research-quantifying-github-copilots-impact-on-developer-productivity-and-happiness/ (accessed 26 February 2025).

2. GitHub Copilot Blog (February 2025). Does GitHub Copilot Improve Code Quality? Here's What the Data Says. https://github.blog/news-insights/research/does-github-copilot-improve-code-quality-heres-what-the-data-says/ (accessed 26 February 2025).

3. Alistair Cockburn, Laurie Williams. The Costs and Benefits of Pair Programming. https://dijkstra.eecs.umich.edu/kleach/eecs481/sp20/readings/pairprogramming.pdf.

4. Via Satellite (February 2019). Microsoft CEO: Every Company is Now a Software Company. https://www.satellitetoday.com/technology/2019/02/26/microsoft-ceo-every-company-is-now-a-software-company/ (accessed 26 February 2025).

5. Korn Ferry Insights (May 2018). The $8.5 Trillion Talent Shortage. https://www.kornferry.com/insights/this-week-in-leadership/talent-crunch-future-of-work (accessed 26 February 2025).

6. Future Code (March 2024). How to Retain Employees in IT? Top Strategies to Attract Software Engineers. https://future-code.dev/en/blog/how-to-retain-employees-in-it-top-strategies-to-attract-software-engineers (accessed 26 February 2025).

7. Stack Overflow (January 2022). Find and retain the best software engineering talent with a strong Employer Brand and Employee Value Proposition. https://stackoverflow.co/advertising/resources/find-and-retain-the-best-software-engineering-talent (accessed 26 February 2025).

8. Microsoft Blog (June 2018). Microsoft to acquire GitHub for $7.5 billion. https://news.microsoft.com/2018/06/04/microsoft-to-acquire-github-for-7-5-billion (accessed 26 February 2025).

9. Benzinga.com (July 2024). Satya Nadella Says Microsoft's Copilot Drives 40% of GitHub's Revenue Growth: We Are Also "Enabling Anyone to Use Natural Language to Create Apps…" https://www.benzinga.com/news/24/07/40061358/satya-nadella-says-microsofts-copilot-drives-40-of-githubs-revenue-growth-we-are-also-enabling-anyon (accessed 26 February 2025).

10. https://github.com/features/copilot
11. GitHub Copilot Blog (January 2023). 100 million Developers and Counting. https://github.blog/news-insights/company-news/100-million-developers-and-counting/ (accessed 26 February 2025).
12. https://reg.githubuniverse.com/flow/github/universe24/attendee-portal/page/sessioncatalog/session/1715273956244001E7G7?browser_session_id=a74ed5e5b181f2fdff41a8182041ca03034f7011198913b72bda6470e65d825d
13. https://www.sap.com/about/company.html
14. https://reg.githubuniverse.com/flow/github/universe24/attendee-portal/page/sessioncatalog/session/1716772047563001o29F
15. Anthropic Blog (June 2024). Claude 3.5 Sonnet. https://www.anthropic.com/news/claude-3-5-sonnet (accessed 26 February 2025).
16. Bito Blog (July 2024). Gemini 1.5 Pro vs GPT-4 Turbo Benchmarks. https://bito.ai/blog/gemini-1-5-pro-vs-gpt-4-turbo-benchmarks (accessed 26 February 2025).

Chapter

3

Differences in GitHub Copilot Versions

THE GITHUB COPILOT EXAM OBJECTIVES COVERED IN THIS CHAPTER INCLUDE, BUT ARE NOT LIMITED TO, THE FOLLOWING:

✔ **Domain 2: GitHub Copilot plans and features**

- Identify the main features with GitHub Copilot Individual
    - Explain the difference between GitHub Copilot Individual and GitHub Copilot Business (data exclusions, IP indemnity, billing, etc.)
    - Understand the available features in the IDE for GitHub Copilot Individual
- Identify the main features of GitHub Copilot Business
    - Demonstrate how to exclude specific files from GitHub Copilot
    - Demonstrate how to establish organization-wide policy management
    - Describe the purpose of organization audit logs for GitHub Copilot Business
    - Explain how to search audit log events for GitHub Copilot Business
    - Explain how to manage GitHub Copilot Business subscriptions via the REST API
- Identify the main features with GitHub Copilot Enterprise
    - Explain the benefits of using GitHub Copilot Chat on GitHub.com
    - Explain GitHub Copilot pull request summaries
    - Explain how to configure and use Knowledge Bases within GitHub Copilot Enterprise

- Describe the different types of knowledge that can be stores in a Knowledge Base (e.g., code snippets, best practices, design patterns)

- Explain the benefits of using Knowledge Bases for code completion and review (e.g., improve code quality, consistency, and efficiency)

- Describe instructions for creating, managing, and searching Knowledge Bases within GitHub Copilot Enterprise, including details on indexing and other relevant configuration steps

- Explain the benefits of using custom models

The four different versions of GitHub Copilot come with many features. If you check out the GitHub Copilot website—at `https://github.com/features/copilot/plans`— you can see that there are several pages that list the capabilities. However, for the exam, you only need to know some of the main differences among the plans, which is what this chapter covers. Just some of these include the ability for data exclusion, audit logs, organization-wide policy management, pull request summaries, and custom models.

GitHub Copilot Individual

In the exam, when the name "GitHub Copilot Individual" is used, it is referring to the Pro edition. Chapter 2 explained the core features of this system, such as chat, inline chat, and code completion. There are also some features that are not covered by the exam, like Edits.

As for the differences between this edition and the Business and Enterprise editions, they are in the following categories:

- AI-native experiences
- Management and policies
- Customization

However, before you look at these, let's first review an important feature that is included in all versions except for the free edition—that is, pull request summaries.

Pull Request Summaries

A *pull request* is a way for developers to propose and collaborate on changes within a codebase. This is done by using a version control system like GitHub or git.

A pull request will often have a description, which can include:

- Summary of the changes
- Rationales for the changes
- Information about the implementation
- Testing that was conducted

Even though pull requests help improve code quality and performance, the process can be tedious. According to an academic study—based on 333,000 pull requests—about 34 percent of them lacked descriptions.[1]

But with GitHub Copilot, you can use AI to create them. To see how this works, Exercise 3.1 shows the steps to take.

EXERCISE 3.1

Creating Pull Request Summaries

1. In VS Code, make some changes to a code file.

2. On the sidebar, click the source control icon. The following graphic shows what you will see. There is a box where you can enter your pull request description.

3. On the right side of the input box is the sparkle icon. Click this icon and the AI will generate a description.

4. Review the description and make any necessary changes.

5. Once you are satisfied with the description, commit it to your repository.

Depending on the number of files, the AI-generated pull request can take more than a minute to generate. This is why there is a limitation of analyzing the first 30 files. Regardless, the feature is still powerful and can be a time saver.

The next section looks at the key differences between the Individual (Pro) edition and the Business and Enterprise editions.

AI-Native Experiences

AI-native experiences are the various features in the IDE that help with certain tasks. For example, with Copilot Individual, you can use slash commands and context variables for your prompts. You can also use this tool to generate a message for pull requests.

Another useful feature is code review for VS Code, which provides a comprehensive analysis. Exercise 3.2 shows the steps for this.

EXERCISE 3.2

Reviewing VS Code

1. Select the code you want to review.

2. Open the VS Code Command Palette. For the Mac, you use Command+Shift+P and for Windows, you use Control+Shift+P.

3. In the input box, search for GitHub Copilot: Review and Comment.

4. The following image shows the analysis.

5. At the top, the code is highlighted, and below are suggestions for changes to make. You can either apply or discard them. In this example, there are three suggestions.

Management and Policies

GitHub Copilot Individual is quite limited for management and policies. But this should not be surprising. The tool is designed for one person, not a team or an organization.

There is one part of management and policies that applies to the Individual edition. It's the public code filter with code referencing. This is a process where GitHub Copilot will identify generated code that matches code in public repositories. This is to avoid the potential of intellectual property violations.

Code referencing applies to code suggestions that are longer than 150 characters. For this, GitHub Copilot will remove all whitespace and compare the result to an index of all public code in GitHub.com. If there is a match, you will get a notification.

In all, the safety process is highly efficient, usually taking less than 300 milliseconds.[2]

The search index for the code referencing is updated only every few months. This means that recent code may not be flagged. At the same time, the code referencing may detect code that has been deleted. In other words, the safety process is not fool-proof. It may miss some of the matches. This is why you should not have the safety feature as the only approach. There should also be a legal review.

The code referencing capability only applies to AI-generated code, such as from code completion or via Copilot Chat. It is not used when you write your own code.

According to GitHub, the matches for code referencing happens in less than 1 percent of the suggestions.[3]

Customization

GitHub Copilot Individual has relatively few customization features. This is essentially a premium capability. Chapter 2 looked at some of the customization features for Copilot Individual. These include using extensions for integrating third-party applications. You can also build your own extensions, which are based on your internal requirements.

Another customization is the use of a markdown file—for example, `copilot-instructions.md`—to provide context for prompts you use for Chat. You store this file in the root of your repository. It will be in the `.github/` folder.

The file will often be coding guidelines, best practices, and standards. You write these in natural language and there is no format required.

Here's an example:

```
Use Django for web development tasks.
Follow PEP 8 guidelines for code formatting.
Use pytest for writing and running tests.
When defining models, inherit from 'models.Model' and include a "__str__" method
for readable representations.
```

Next, you can create prompt files, which allow you to reuse prompt instructions. This is also a markdown file. There are many use cases, including tests, forms, and API mocks. You can also use prompt files for sharing security practices, documentation, and specifications.

The naming convention is to use a descriptive name for the prompt and add `-.prompt.md`. You will then place this in the `.github/prompts` folder of your repository.

Consider this example. Suppose you commonly use data validation for your forms. You use the `data-validation.prompt.md` filename for it.

For this validation, you use natural language. Here is an example:

```
# Data Validation Function

Your task is to create a data validation function in Python.

Requirements:
- The function should accept a dictionary representing user input.
- Validate the following fields:
  - "username":
    - Must be a non-empty string.
    - Length between 3 and 20 characters.
```

```
          - Can contain alphanumeric characters and underscores only.
    - "email":
      - Must be a valid email address format.
    - "age":
      - Must be an integer between 18 and 99.
  - Return a tuple:
    - A boolean indicating if the input is valid.
    - A list of error messages for any invalid fields.
```

Use Python's 're' module for regex validation and include appropriate error handling.

To use this, you click the attach icon in Chat and then select Prompt. You will then select `data-validation.prompt.md`. You can use a prompt like this:

@workspace Please create a data validation function as described in data-validation. prompt.md.

GitHub Copilot Business

When compared to GitHub Copilot Individual, the Business edition has the same features for AI-native experiences and customization. The differences are mainly with management and policies. Another benefit is that there is centralized billing as well as access control and identity for security purposes.

But before looking at these, you need to understand what an *organization* is. This is a shared entity—in GitHub.com—where you can collaborate on many projects. The organization will also benefit from strong security and administrative features.

Exercise 3.3 shows the steps for creating an organization.

EXERCISE 3.3

Creating an Organization

1. Log in to GitHub.com.

2. On the top right of the screen, click the + icon.

3. Choose New Organization.

4. Select the GitHub plan that is best for your needs.

5. Enter the name of your organization and the billing email.

6. You can add team members to the organization.

7. Select Create Organization.

The next section looks at the other management and policy options.

User Management

User management allows you to grant access to GitHub Copilot. For any user—or seat—this is also included in your subscription. There is no need to buy a certain number of seats upfront. When you revoke a seat, this will also reduce the subscription.

Exercise 3.4 illustrates how to add seats to an organization.

EXERCISE 3.4

Adding Seats

1. Click your profile, which is on the top-right part of the screen on GitHub.com.

2. Click Organizations and then choose Settings, which is on the right side of the screen.

3. On the sidebar, select Copilot and then click Access.

4. Select Starting Adding Seats. A drop-down will show two options. You can either purchase seats for all members or for selected members.

5. You then go through the billing process.

Before adding and configuring seats, it's important to have a strategy. If not, you can easily create a system that is difficult to manage, does not meet your needs, and can lead to higher costs. For example, if the goal is to have as many developers as possible using the GitHub policy, the best approach may be to assign seats for the entire organization or according to an identity provider (IdP) group. This provides a single set of access credentials across multiple platforms. This helps with security and user convenience, such as through an identify provider like Microsoft Entra ID or Okta.

On the other hand, if you want a more customized environment, you should spend more time on the planning. You can then map this to the organization settings. You can also use the GitHub Copilot REST API, which allows you to create an application to automate the process. The data is maintained for the last 28 days.

There are two main endpoints for the API:

- **Subscription management:** You can assign seats for specific users or teams. This will seamlessly provide the adjustments for billing. You can also automatically revoke access, by setting seats to "pending cancellation." They will be removed at the end of the billing cycle.

- **Usage metrics:** This provides daily aggregated details, such as on the number of code completions, chat interactions, and active users. There are breakdowns according to programming languages and the IDEs.

Data Exclusion

GitHub Copilot for Business allows you to configure the system to ignore certain files for code completion and chat responses. A GitHub repository administrator can exclude the content. The actions are applied to any of the Copilot users working in the affected repositories. As for organization owners, they can exclude content for users based on seats in an organization.

Regardless of the control, the exclusion process is the same. The IDE will send the URL for the excluded files to the GitHub server. But they are not logged, so as to allow for more privacy.

But GitHub Copilot still may use the information indirectly. For example, if your IDE provides details like type information or symbol definitions from an excluded file, it could use this data in its responses. This can also include project details like build configurations.

Exercise 3.5 shows the steps for excluding content from repositories.

EXERCISE 3.5

Excluding Content from Repositories

1. Go to a repository on GitHub.com that is a part of an organization.

2. At the top of the screen, select Settings.

3. On the sidebar, click Copilot. You will see the following screen.

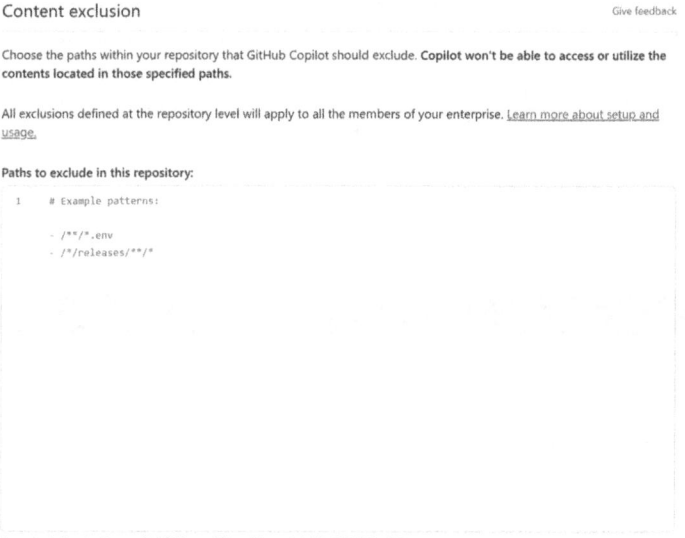

4. Where it says Paths to Exclude in This Repository, enter the paths you want excluded. Each path must be on a separate line. You can also add comments with #.

IP Indemnity

In late 2022, a group of plaintiffs filed a class-action lawsuit against GitHub, Microsoft, and OpenAI.[4] The allegation was that these companies were violating open-source licenses because of the AI-generated code.

The legal issues were complex, and the litigation was time-consuming and expensive. But even if defendants would ultimately defeat the lawsuit, this may not have been enough. Customers of GitHub Copilot had legitimate concerns that they could be vulnerable to legal liability.

To address this, the defendants announced a novel solution: intellectual property indemnity (IP). This is a legal obligation to compensate customers for the losses for litigation over infringement. It became a safeguard for GitHub Copilot Business and Enterprise editions.

This certainly allayed many fears. After all, Microsoft, GitHub, and OpenAI have substantial amounts of resources. Although, to get the protection, an organization would need to enable the duplicate detection filter.

However, IP indemnity is a specialized area of the law. So it is important to make sure legal counsel reviews any of the issues for your organization.

Audit Logs

Audit logs are chronological records that track activities and tasks in GitHub Copilot. They help provide accountability, improved security, troubleshooting and forensic analysis.

For GitHub Copilot, the audit logs provide details about changes to the settings and policies, as well as the addition and removal of seats from subscriptions. This data is maintained for the last 180 days.

Exercise 3.6 shows how to access the audit logs.

EXERCISE 3.6

Accessing the Audit Logs

1. Click your profile photo at the top right of the screen and then select Your Organization.

2. At the top of the screen, select Settings.

3. On the sidebar, choose Logs at the bottom and then select Audit Log. You will see the following screen.

Audit log

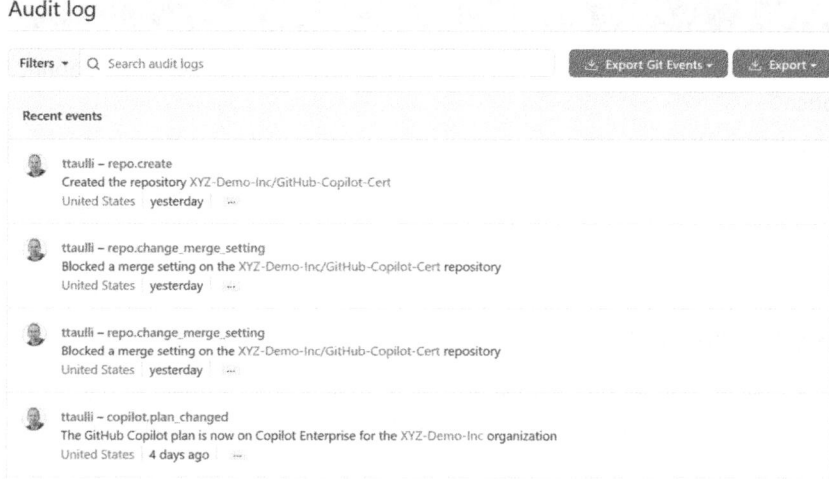

4. At the top of the screen, click Filters. You will see the different options, such as to search for Copilot activity. There are other filters, such as type, date, and user actions.

5. In the search box, you can use qualifiers to refine the search. For example, if you want to see audit logs for Copilot, you use `action:copilot`.

GitHub Copilot Enterprise

Compared to Copilot Business, the Enterprise edition adds features like knowledge bases and customization for code review. However, before looking at these, this section covers how to set up this application.

First, you need to subscribe to the GitHub Enterprise Cloud, and this cannot be the trial version. You must start the paid edition. Otherwise, you can only have GitHub Copilot Business.

After you activate GitHub Enterprise Cloud, you will add details about your enterprise and invite existing members to join. This allows for centralizing the management of repositories and teams.

To install GitHub Copilot Enterprise, you then follow the steps in Exercise 3.7.

EXERCISE 3.7

Installing GitHub Copilot Enterprise

1. Click your profile photo at the top right of the screen and then select Your Enterprises option. You will then choose the enterprise you want.

2. In the sidebar, select Policies and then click Copilot.

3. Where it says Copilot Business is Active in Your Enterprise, click Purchase Copilot Enterprise.

4. Select Continue to Billing Summary.

5. Click Enable Plan.

Knowledge Bases

A *knowledge base* in GitHub Copilot Enterprise is a collection of files—in markdown format—that are in one or more repositories for an organization. You use this to provide more context when using Copilot Chat, such as in an IDE or GitHub.com.

Here are some of the types of files you can use for knowledge bases:

- **Code samples:** These are for common functions and methods, say for logins or integrations.

- **Best practices:** These are guidelines for efficient and effective coding standards for an organization. An example is an outline of the preferred error-handling mechanisms in your codebase.

- **Design patterns:** This is for handling recurring design issues. For example, there could be an explanation of the Singleton pattern. This could have scenarios where it's beneficial and sample implementations.

- **API documentation:** You can include the whole file, showing the examples, definitions, and response structures.

- **Style guides:** These are the internal rules and conventions for writing code.

Knowledge bases can be quite beneficial for software development, as they can provide a richer level of customization.

Here are some of the other advantages:

- **Improved code quality:** GitHub Copilot will create code suggestions that are in line with your organization's best practices and methods.

- **Consistency:** Without knowledge bases, the output of GitHub Copilot can vary in terms of style and form. This is largely due to the diversity of the underlying datasets for the LLM. But with knowledge bases, the AI-generated code will be much more uniform. This will help provide for maintainability of the codebase.

- **Efficiency and productivity:** There will be much less time needed to search for information in documentation. Also, developers who are not familiar with an organization's coding standards will be able to get up to speed faster with their development.

Creating and Using a Knowledge Base

You can create a knowledge base for one or more repositories. They can be public, private, or internal. But knowledge bases are available only to those who have a GitHub Copilot seat and belong to the relevant organization.

Exercise 3.8 shows the steps for creating a knowledge base.

EXERCISE 3.8

Creating a Knowledge Base

1. Click your profile photo on the top right of the screen for GitHub.com.

2. Select Your Organizations and then choose Settings.

3. In the sidebar, click Copilot and then choose Knowledge Bases.

4. Click New Knowledge Base. You will see the following screen.

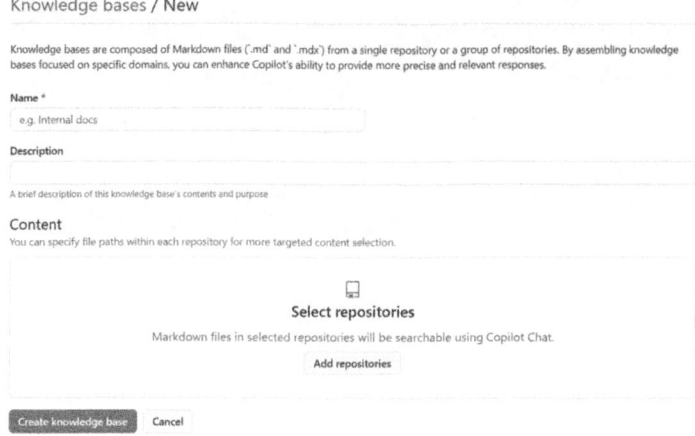

5. For the Name field, enter something descriptive and unique. You can also provide more details about the knowledge base in the Description field.

6. Click Add Repositories, which will have access to the knowledge bases. You will see a drop-down of them. Choose the repositories you want.

7. Select Create Knowledge Base. This process is called *indexing*. That is, GitHub is detecting the markdown files and integrating them into a knowledge base. The process can take a few minutes, depending on the size of the repository.

Next, let's look at how to use this knowledge base in VS Code. Exercise 3.9 shows the steps.

EXERCISE 3.9

Using Knowledge Bases in VS Code

1. Click the Copilot icon on the top right of the screen.

2. Select Open Chat.

3. Enter **@github**.

4. Enter **#**. You will see a drop-down, such as the one shown here.

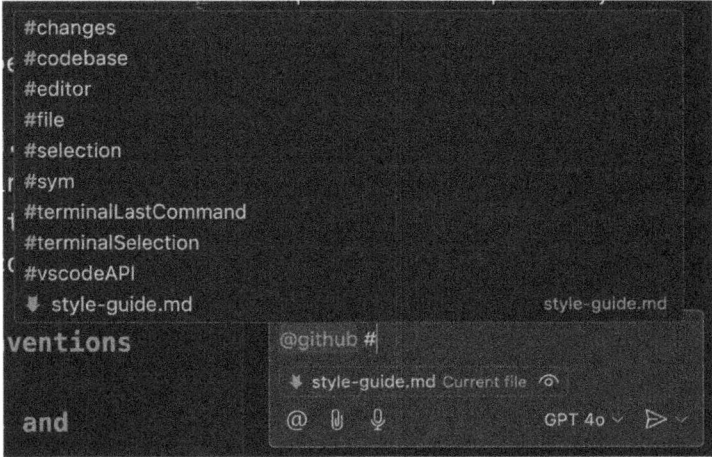

5. Choose the knowledge base.

6. Enter the rest of your prompt, such as to generate code. The response will use the knowledge base as context.

Custom Models

A *custom model* is a way to fine-tune the LLM of GitHub Copilot. This allows you to tailor the AI for the particular requirements and coding standards of your organization.

Building a custom model involves the following steps:

1. **Preparing the repositories:** You select those that reflect your organization's processes, methods, and standards. These will be proprietary libraries, internal frameworks, and specialized languages.

2. **Telemetry collection:** GitHub recommends enabling this. It will allow for better customization.

3. **Training:** GitHub will handle this process. After this is complete, your organization can select the custom model for code development.

4. **Monitoring:** It's important to track the performance of the custom model, which you can do using the GitHub Copilot REST API.

Custom models can be more effective than other techniques, such as specifying files or using knowledge bases. The reason is that there are adjustments of the parameters of the LLM.

Some of the other benefits include:

- **Quality:** There should be fewer errors because of the high level of customization.

- **Personalization:** If you work with specialized systems and languages, a custom model can allow for much better results. The custom model will essentially be tailored for the nuances and intricacies.

- **Speed:** Since the model is fine-tuned, this means the responses will be faster. There is no need to look up various files.

- **Privacy:** The data you use in the training is yours. It's not used for the custom models of other customers.

- **Adaptability:** You can easily update the custom model. This allows it to remain relevant as your organization's requirements evolve.

The Key Differences

The chapter has covered many features across the different versions of GitHub Copilot. So for the exam, what should you focus on?

Keep in mind that all the material is fair game. It's part of what is available in the study guide. But to help make learning the differences easier, Table 3.1 lists the key features included in each version.

TABLE 3.1   Key Features in GitHub Copilot Versions

Feature	Description	GitHub Copilot Version
Pull requests	Copilot analyzes code changes and generates a natural language summary to provide an overview of the modifications.	Individual (Pro), Business, Enterprise
Exclude files from GitHub Copilot	Organization administrators can exclude specific files from Copilot by adding file paths to the organization's settings.	Business, Enterprise

(*Continued*)

TABLE 3.1   (Continued)

Feature	Description	GitHub Copilot Version
Audit logs	Chronological records that track activities and tasks in GitHub Copilot. This helps with compliance, security, and troubleshooting. Audit logs are searchable by event type, date, and user action.	Business, Enterprise
GitHub Copilot REST API	Used for automating and configuring policies at the organization level, managing user licenses, and retrieving repository-specific usage analytics.	Business, Enterprise
Knowledge bases	Stores design patterns, best practices, and reusable code snippets. This helps improve code quality, consistency, and efficiency.	Enterprise
Custom models	Fine-tuned LLM models customized for an organization's coding standards. This helps improve accuracy, personalization, and efficiency.	Enterprise

Summary

This chapter looked at the main differences among the four plans for GitHub Copilot. They include data exclusions, audit logs, pull request summaries, and custom models.

The next chapter covers how GitHub Copilot handles data, such as with code completions and chat.

Exam Essentials

Understand pull request summaries.   These use GitHub Copilot's LLM to generate pull requests. They are based on the relevant repositors. The system will evaluate up to 30 files.

Learn about excluding data from being processed by GitHub Copilot.   You can exclude certain files from being accessed. This is done by changing the settings and specifying the file paths.

Know how audit logs work.   They monitor activities in GitHub Copilot. This can help improve compliance, security, and troubleshooting. The audit logs are provided at an organization level. They can also be searched by using various filters.

Understand the GitHub Copilot REST API.   This gives you access to usage patterns at a repository level. This can be used to create applications to automate processes, such as to evaluate an organization's effectiveness with GitHub Copilot or helping to improve compliance. You can also use the REST API for managing subscriptions, such as with assignments and revocations.

Learn about knowledge bases.   These allow for embedding data into GitHub Copilot to improve its customization. This is done at an organization level. The information for knowledge bases can include many sources, like code snippets, best practices, and documentation. Some of the benefits are improved code reviews and code quality.

Understand custom models.   This is where you fine-tune the GitHub Copilot LLM. This provides a high level of customization, such as for your coding standards, procedures, and patterns.

Review Questions

1. Which feature is exclusive to GitHub Copilot Enterprise?

    A. Pull request summaries

    B. Organization-wide policy management

    C. Knowledge bases

    D. Inline code suggestions

2. Which of the following is a unique feature of GitHub Copilot Business compared to the Individual version?

    A. Centralized billing

    B. Inline code suggestions

    C. Chat integration in the IDE

    D. Pull request summaries

3. What is the main advantage of using custom models in GitHub Copilot Enterprise?

    A. They allow unlimited usage across all repositories.

    B. They provide improved accuracy and efficiency by tailoring the model to organizational coding standards.

    C. They automatically fix syntax errors in code.

    D. They replace the need for knowledge bases.

4. How does GitHub Copilot generate pull request summaries?

    A. By comparing the pull request to similar ones in the repository history

    B. By analyzing the changes and creating a natural language summary

    C. By running test cases on the modified code and reporting results

    D. By listing all filenames and code lines changed

5. Which of the following is true about audit logs in GitHub Copilot Business?

    A. They allow developers to view code completion suggestions.

    B. They are only accessible to repository contributors.

    C. They track activities and policy changes for compliance and security.

    D. They automatically assign seats for new team members.

6. What is a key benefit of using knowledge bases in GitHub Copilot Enterprise?

    A. Enhancing code quality with shared best practices

    B. They are only accessible to repository contributors

    C. Automatically fixing runtime errors

    D. Allowing unlimited repository usage

7. Which GitHub Copilot version supports organization-wide policy management?

    A. Copilot Individual

    B. Copilot Pro

    C. Copilot Business

    D. Copilot Chat

8. Which of the following is not a feature of GitHub Copilot Individual?

    A. Inline code suggestions

    B. Custom models

    C. Pull request summaries

    D. Slash commands and context variables for prompts

9. How can administrators exclude specific files from GitHub Copilot Business?

    A. By creating a `.copilotignore` file in each repository

    B. By removing the files from the repository

    C. By disabling Copilot for the entire organization

    D. By adding file paths to the organization's Copilot settings

10. What is a unique feature of GitHub Copilot Enterprise compared to the Business version?

    A. Organization-wide policy management

    B. Knowledge bases for enhanced code completion

    C. Centralized billing for teams

    D. Inline code suggestions with context awareness

11. Which GitHub Copilot version provides IP indemnity for generated code?

    A. Copilot Individual

    B. Copilot Pro

    C. Copilot Business

    D. Copilot Chat

12. In GitHub Copilot Business, how can an administrator manage seat assignments?

    A. Through the IDE settings panel

    B. Using the GitHub REST API for subscription management

    C. By creating a `.copilotignore` file

    D. By directly editing the repository's permissions

13. Which feature in GitHub Copilot helps prevent the use of public code without proper licensing?

    A. Inline code suggestions

    B. Knowledge bases

    C. Public code filter with code referencing

    D. Custom models

14. What is a primary use case for the GitHub Copilot REST API?

    A. Automating seat assignments and revocations

    B. Generating pull request summaries

    C. Creating custom models for code completion

    D. Running real-time syntax checks

15. Which feature is common between GitHub Copilot Business and Enterprise, but not available in Individual?

    A. Custom models

    B. Inline code suggestions

    C. Organization-wide content exclusions

    D. Slash commands for prompts

16. How can administrators search for specific events in GitHub Copilot Business audit logs?

    A. By using a `.gitignore` file in the repository

    B. By exporting CSV reports from GitHub support

    C. By querying with filters like event type or date range

    D. Directly from the IDE's configuration panel

17. Which is a benefit of using pull request summaries in GitHub Copilot?

    A. Automatically resolving merge conflicts

    B. Generating a natural language overview of code changes

    C. Providing inline code suggestions without context

    D. Archiving all previous pull request versions

18. What is the purpose of centralized billing in GitHub Copilot Business?

    A. To provide free unlimited repositories

    B. To allow individual users to manage their own subscriptions

    C. To enable custom model integration

    D. To streamline payment management for organizations

19. Which feature in GitHub Copilot Business helps organizations comply with data privacy regulations?

    A. Inline code suggestions

    B. Organization-wide content exclusions

    C. Real-time syntax error checking

    D. Unlimited repository access

20. In GitHub Copilot Enterprise, how are knowledge bases created and managed?

    A. By storing markdown files in selected repositories

    B. By using `.copilotignore` files in each repository

    C. Through inline commands in the IDE

    D. By exporting repository data to an external database

Notes

1. Arxiv (September 2019). Automatic Generation of Pull Request Descriptions. https://arxiv.org/abs/1909.06987 (accessed 26 February 2025).

2. https://reg.githubuniverse.com/flow/github/universe24/attendee-portal/page/sessioncatalog/session/1715178970303001Gg0A?browser_session_id=a74ed5e5b181f2fdff41a8182041ca03034f7011198913b72bda6470e65d825d

3. GitHub Docs (2025). Finding Public Code that Matches GitHub Copilot Suggestions. https://docs.github.com/en/copilot/using-github-copilot/finding-public-code-that-matches-github-copilot-suggestions (accessed 26 February 2025).

4. Joseph Saveri Law Firm Blog. GitHub and Copilot Intellectual Property Litigation. https://www.saverilawfirm.com/our-cases/github-copilot-intellectual-property-litigation (accessed 26 February 2025).

Chapter

4

The Role of Data

THE GITHUB COPILOT EXAM OBJECTIVES COVERED IN THIS CHAPTER INCLUDE, BUT ARE NOT LIMITED TO, THE FOLLOWING:

✔ **Domain 3: How GitHub Copilot works and handles data**

- Describe how GitHub Copilot handles data
  - Describe how the data in GitHub Copilot individual is used and shared
  - Explain the data flow for GitHub Copilot code completion
  - Explain the data flow for GitHub Copilot Chat
  - Describe the different types of input processing for GitHub Copilot Chat (types of prompts it was designed for)
- Describe the data pipeline lifecycle of GitHub Copilot code suggestions in the IDE
  - Visualize the lifecycle of a GitHub Copilot code suggestion
  - Explain how GitHub Copilot gathers context
  - Explain how GitHub Copilot builds a prompt
  - Describe the proxy service and the filters each prompt goes through
  - Describe how the large language model produces its response
  - Explain the post-processing of GitHub Copilot's responses through the proxy server
  - Identify how GitHub Copilot identifies matching code
- Describe the limitations of GitHub Copilot (and LLMs in general)
  - Describe the effect of most seen examples on the source data
  - Describe the age of code suggestions (how old and relevant the data is)
  - Describe the nature of GitHub Copilot providing reasoning and context from a prompt vs calculations
  - Describe limited context windows

This chapter focuses on how GitHub Copilot handles data. The first couple sections, though, are not covered on the exam. The purpose of this information is to give you a general overview of data—such as the major trends driving the growth—as well as the challenges you may experience. You will then learn about the critical data flows in an LLM.

The rest of the chapter covers topics that will likely show up on the exam. You will learn about data security, including the various precautions that GitHub Copilot provides. This includes important details about how data works in the Individual edition. You'll learn about the importance of steps like prompt crafting, model processing, post-processing, and safety.

Finally, you'll look at some of the data limitations with GitHub Copilot and LLMs.

The World of Data

The amount of data in the world is enormous. It is also growing at a rapid pace. In 2024, the global data creation hit about 149 *zettabytes (ZB)*, translating to roughly 0.4 zettabytes per day.[1] To put this into perspective, global data creation came to about 64.2 zettabytes in 2020 and was only 6.5 zettabytes in 2012.[2]

So what is a zettabyte? It can actually be tough to comprehend, but it's one trillion gigabytes or one sextillion bytes. If you streamed Netflix continuously for 36 million years, this would be a zettabyte of HD video.

In a way, this data growth should not necessarily be surprising. After all, there are many factors driving it:

- **Smartphones:** There are more than 7 billion in the world, representing about 90 percent of the population. On average, they use about 20 GB of data each month.[3]

- **Social media platforms:** They generate massive amounts of text, audio, and video content. Consider that more than 5 billion people are active on social media platforms.[4] Even smaller ones can generate large amounts of data. For example, users on Snapchat share more than 500,000 photos every minute.[5]

- **Video streaming:** This consumes large amounts of data, especially when using 4K video. Video represents 82.5 percent of global Internet traffic.[6]

- **AI:** Increasingly, content is AI-generated. Studies estimate it at 57 percent, and this could reach 90 percent by 2026.[7]

- **IoT (Internet-of-Things) devices:** These include Internet-enabled systems like home wearables, industrial sensors, and smart appliances. An estimate shows that IoT data will reach 80 ZB by 2025.[8]

All this data requires major investments in infrastructure, such as datacenters. Of course, the biggest players in the market are Microsoft, Meta, Google, and Amazon. In 2025, they have indicated that they will spend a whopping $215 billion for IT infrastructure, up 45 percent on a year-over-year basis.[9]

This has also included the need for investing in energy sources. In 2023, datacenters accounted for 4.4 percent of total electricity in the United States, according to the Department of Energy. But by 2028, the estimate is for 6.7 to 12 percent.[10]

To deal with this growth, large tech companies have been strategic with their datacenters. They are generally located near areas with energy sources, like solar or wind power stations.

But this can go only so far. This is why there has been renewed interest in nuclear energy. For example, in November 2024, Microsoft entered a partnership with Constellation Energy to restart the reactor in Pennsylvania's Three Mile Island (in 1979, it suffered the worst nuclear accident in U.S. history). Microsoft agreed to invest $1.6 billion in the project.[11]

To say that data is the "new oil" does seem apt. It is becoming a highly strategic asset. It is also core to AI. As covered in Chapter 1, data is used for the training models. For the most advanced models, the datasets can be huge.

To get a sense of this, look at the evolution of Meta's Llama model, which is open-source. The training data is as follows:[12]

- Llama 1 (February 2023): 1.4 trillion tokens
- Llama 2 (July 2023): 2 trillion tokens
- Llama 3 (April 2024): 15 trillion tokens

But the quantity is only one part of the equation. The data also needs to be high quality. This is certainly critical for tools like GitHub Copilot. As they are being used for more critical applications, there needs to be high levels of accuracy and relevancy.

Not Enough Data?

In light of the large amount of data that's created every day, it seems strange that there are concerns that we are running out. But it does look like this is a legitimate concern—at least when it comes to quality data.

Some academic studies predict that we'll start running out of new training data for AI models in 2026.[13] If so, this could hinder AI development. For example, the models may be less effective in terms of generating useful or accurate content.

It's true that there are advanced techniques to improve data quality. But they can be time consuming, manual, and expensive. As datasets get larger and larger, it's not as practical to use optimizations.

Given this, there are already signs of diminishing returns for new LLMs. When new models are released, the improvements are often incremental. In some cases, it can be tough to discern any overall difference.[14]

Another way to help with the data scarcity problem is to use synthetic data, which is generated by AI. It has shown to be effective with narrow use cases, such as to deal with outliers and gaps. But there are still issues. It's not uncommon for synthetic data to lead to degradation of effectiveness over time.

But there is another emerging issue: when an AI model is trained, more of the data is AI-generated. This results in an interesting feedback loop. It's not clear what the ramifications are, but some researchers think it could result in faulty models. There may even be the potential for "model collapse."

All in all, there are various risk factors for the advancement of AI—and much of this is due to data. The good news is that there is much research being focused on these matters. There will likely be breakthroughs, but in the meantime, it could mean that there is some disappointment in the progress with this technology.

Data Flows in LLM Development

When looking at how data works with GitHub Copilot, it's good to get an understanding of the flows in the development cycle of an LLM. The steps can vary, and some of the details are opaque. But generally, they include the following:

- Problem framing
- Data collection
- Data preprocessing
- Training of the model
- Model deployment and monitoring

The following sections look at each of these steps.

Problem Framing

It may seem simple, but the first step in creating an AI model is to set a goal. Basically, what problem is to be solved?

In the case of an LLM for an AI coding system, this is often quite ambitious. Consider that this is the vision for OpenAI:[15]

> "OpenAI's mission is to ensure that artificial general intelligence (AGI)—by which we mean highly autonomous systems that outperform humans at most economically valuable work—benefits all of humanity."

As you learned in Chapter 1, these models can be extremely expensive to build and require huge amounts of data. They involve highly qualified data scientists, who usually have strong academic backgrounds. But there are also data engineers and architects. Finding and attracting this talent is no easy feat. The compensation packages can sometimes be in the seven figures.

But another trend is toward *small language models (SLMs)*, which are a fraction of the size of LLMs. They can still be quite powerful and fast, allowing for better real-time interactions. They are also usually open-source, which provides for more transparency and customization. In the years ahead, SLMs are likely to become more popular for AI coding because of these advantages. In fact, Meta's own SLMs—which are part of the Llama series—have proven to be quite capable.

Data Collection

In a way, the data collection process is fairly straightforward for an LLM. It's about collecting all the publicly available data from the Internet. Modern scraping techniques actually make this easier—as seen with traditional search engines like Google—and storage is relatively cheap.

But there is substantial amounts of data that is behind paywalls, such as from *The New York Times*, the *Wall Street Journal*, and the *Washington Post*. Because of this, the major LLM developers have been licensing this type of content to train their LLMs.

Finally, there is user-generated data. Major LLM developers will hire employees to create content. Applications like ChatGPT and Claude can also be sources of user-generated content, such as from user feedback.

Data Preprocessing

Data is always messy. This is especially true when the dataset includes most of the Internet. To help improve the quality, there is *data preprocessing*.

First, there is the cleaning of the data. This involves removing outliers, duplications, and missing information. The process can be tedious and time-consuming. But there are companies like Scale AI that specialize in data cleaning. They have large numbers of employees who help with the process and also leverage sophisticated automation systems.

Next, data preprocessing will usually include filtering. This involves stripping harmful, toxic, or illegal content from the dataset.

Another important step is tokenization. As you saw in Chapter 1, this is about turning data into a form that the transformer models can process.

Training the Model

Training the model involves processing the dataset with AI algorithms to help it learn patterns. In the case of an LLM, the focus is on how to generate content, whether it be text, audio, code, or video.

This is done using unsupervised learning, because the dataset is unlabeled. The transformer model will analyze the information to understand the underlying relationships.

In most cases, the first version of the training is far from useful. There needs to be ongoing *fine-tuning* of the model to improve its performance. Part of this involves *Reinforcement Learning from Human Feedback* (RLHF). This is where people evaluate the responses of the LLM.

The training process can take months and be expensive. There is also a need to use expensive chips like GPUs (graphics processing units) and TPUs (tensor processing units). To get a sense of the importance of these systems, look at the multibillion-dollar investments in OpenAI and Anthropic. A large proportion of the investments were not in the form of cash but instead access to GPUs and TPUs as well as cloud computing resources.

Model Deployment and Monitoring

After the model is created and vetted, it's time to put it into production. Usually, this is done on one of the large cloud platforms like Azure, AWS, or Google Cloud. They have the necessary capacity, state-of-the-art systems and scalability. Then there are the stringent security and compliance protections.

The rest of this chapter looks deeper into how data impacts tools like GitHub Copilot.

Data Security

A key advantage for GitHub Copilot is that it operates in the cloud, which leverages Microsoft Azure's massive platform. It has a highly scalable platform that spans the globe. Azure also allows for efficiencies and lower costs for GitHub Copilot.

But there is something that can raise concerns: some user data is processed in the cloud. Is this secure? It certainly helps that Azure invests huge amounts of money to protect its systems in the following ways:

- **Physical security:** The Azure datacenters have multiple layers of physical security. This includes perimeter defenses (strong fencing), guards, surveillance cameras and sensors, screenings, and biometric scans for building access.

- **Independent host:** GitHub Copilot is on a dedicated Azure Cloud environment. This is where all user data is processed. This setup provides data isolation from the rest of Azure.

- **Data encryption:** Azure encrypts data at rest, in transit, and in use. *Encryption* is where data is readable by using a private key, which is a long list of numbers (it's like a password).

- **Cybersecurity systems:** Azure invests in the latest tools, such as firewalls and intrusion protection.

- **Security experts:** Azure has thousands of cybersecurity personnel who help with managing systems, monitoring threats, fixing problems, and researching security trends.

- **AI:** Azure uses this technology to enhance its security, which can help detect complex threats and respond quickly. There is also an AI-powered vulnerability prevention system to block insecure coding patterns in real-time while GitHub Copilot generates responses. The system focuses on common vulnerabilities like hard-coded credentials, SQL injections, and path injections. By using LLMs, it mimics the functionality of static analysis tools and can identify risky patterns even in partial code fragments.

Besides the Azure infrastructure, there is the security for GitHub itself, which is also robust. The company has been certified for string requirements like SOC 1 Type 2, SOC 2 Type 2, and IAASB International Standards. There are also certifications for government use cases. Then there is the GitHub Security Lab, which includes a group of security experts that helps promote security for open-source software.

GitHub Copilot also uses a *proxy filter*. This is a server that acts as an intermediary between a user's device and the Internet. This helps block unwanted content or protect sensitive information.

Keep the following in mind:

- If the proxy filter blocks the request, GitHub Copilot won't receive the data. This will mean there will be a failure in the code completion. You may also receive an error message.

- If the proxy removes personal information or questionable content from the request but allows it to proceed, GitHub Copilot can process the modified request and generate suggestions as usual.

Next, there may be a situation when you are working in an *air-gapped environment.* This describes when a computer or network is physically isolated from unsecured networks like the public Internet. GitHub Copilot for Business requires an active Internet connection between the user's IDE and the GitHub Copilot Proxy service to function. As a result, Copilot cannot operate in air-gapped environments where external network access is restricted or entirely blocked.

However, there is another level of security. After all, GitHub Copilot relies on various partners. Some examples include the LLM providers like OpenAI and Anthropic. Each has its own security measures.

Through this ecosystem, there are certainly many safeguards. But security is never perfect—and yes, there are inevitably breaches. According to the FBI's Internet Crime Complaint Center, there were over 880,000 threats reported in the United States in 2023, up 10 percent on a year-over-year basis.[16] The average cost of a breach, according to an IBM study, is $4.88 million.[17]

This is why it's important for any organization to have strong security policies and systems.

Here are some best practices to keep in mind when working with GitHub Copilot:

- **Security review:** Always review code suggestions. There could be vulnerabilities like SQL injections or hard-coded secrets. You should also use a security scan, which helps detect issues and offer fixes.

- **Avoid sharing sensitive information**: In your prompts, do not include any information you would not want to be made publicly available. This should be according to your organization's privacy policies.

- **Use GitHub Copilot's privacy settings:** There is much configuration available, such as for disabling certain features. You will learn more about this in Chapter 7.

- **Stay informed:** Periodically check GitHub's privacy statements to see how GitHub Copilot handles data.

- **Secure your development environment:** Use strong passwords, use multifactor authentication (MFA), and do not work on unsecure networks.

- **Use separate accounts:** You should not use the same account for personal and professional use with GitHub Copilot. Otherwise, you could be exposed to more security vulnerabilities.

Data in GitHub Copilot Individual

The GitHub Copilot certification exam may have questions about how it handles data for individual subscribers. For example, when you write prompts, they will be transmitted to GitHub's servers for the LLMs for processing. However, once a reply is provided, the data is discarded. GitHub does not retain this information for training its own LLMs, which is primarily for privacy reasons. But if you want, you can opt in to allow this. You can see the steps for this process in Exercise 4.1.

EXERCISE 4.1

Opting In for LLM Training

1. In the upper-right of the screen in GitHub.com, select your profile.

2. Select Your Copilot.

3. You will see the settings page shown here.

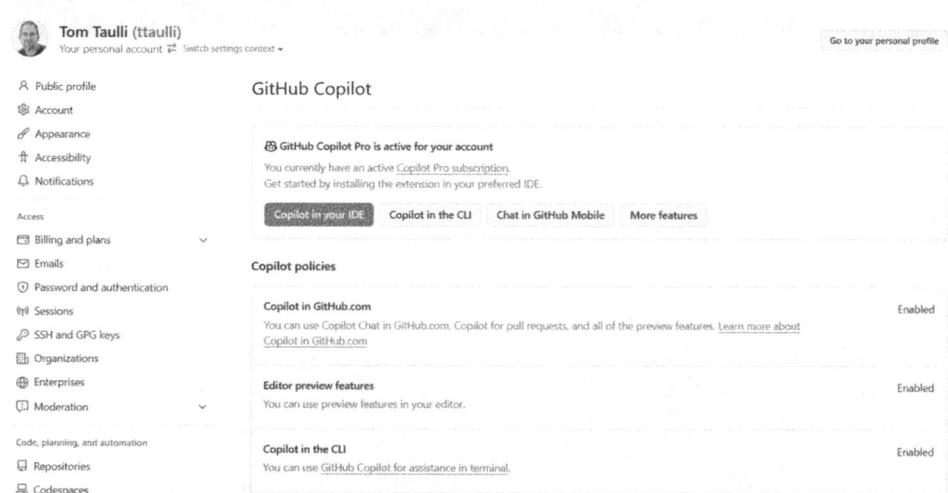

4. Scroll down the page and select the opt-in option for Allow GitHub to Use My Data for Product Improvements.

For individual subscribers of GitHub Copilot, there are other types of data it handles. They include telemetry data, contextual information, and user feedback.

Telemetry Data

Telemetry data is information about the performance of the GitHub Copilot platform. This includes the following:

- **Interaction events:** These are interactions with GitHub Copilot. An example is when you accept or discard a code suggestion.
- **Feature usage:** This is information about the features you use and the frequency of use.
- **Metrics:** This shows the speed of the suggestions.
- **Error logs:** These are reports of errors or issues.

GitHub Copilot anonymizes and aggregates telemetry data. But it is also used to understand usage patterns and improve the performance of the system.

If you want to adjust the settings for telemetry data, you can do this in VS Code, as you can see in Exercise 4.2.

EXERCISE 4.2

Changing the Configuration of Telemetry Data

1. Select the gear icon on the bottom left of the IDE.

2. Click Settings.

3. On the top of the middle of the screen, enter **telemetry** where it says Search Settings.

4. You'll see the screen depicted here.

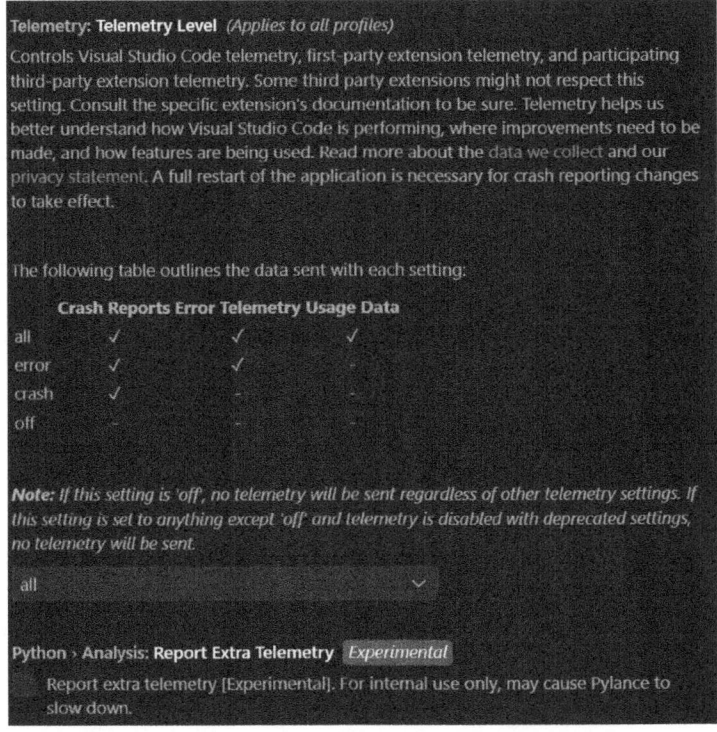

5. At the bottom of the screen, there is a drop-down. You can select the options for the telemetry data. You can select Off to prevent all of it from being used. Or you can choose different types of telemetry not to use, such as for errors or crash analytics.

6. After you make your selections, restart your IDE.

VS Code is not the only system that will collect telemetry information. It's common for third-party extensions to do so as well. They may also not be included in the telemetry settings. Because of this, you need to read the documentation for the extension to see the data policies and the configuration options.

Contextual Information

Contextual information is data about your development environment. This includes:

- **File data:** This is data about the active file in your IDE.
- **Related files:** These are related files for your project.
- **Repository data:** This is data about the repository you're working in, such as file paths and repository URLs.

    This information allows the code suggestions to be more relevant and accurate.

User Feedback

User feedback includes ratings, comments, and reports about incorrect or inappropriate responses from GitHub Copilot. This data can be used to fine-tune the LLM algorithms.

Data Flow for GitHub Copilot

Code completion leverages a sophisticated system to handle the flow of data. It involves four major steps, which you can see in Figure 4.1. They are prompt crafting, model processing, post-processing, and safety.

Prompt Crafting

A prompt is more than your input into an LLM. GitHub Copilot will also add to it, which is done by processing the following:

- **In-file context:** This involves analyzing the code immediately preceding and following the cursor in the active file. It includes snippets of code from open tabs that are in the same programming language.
- **Metadata:** This has the details for file paths and the programming language in use. Metadata will also include related files for the project. With this, GitHub will try to get a better understanding of the codebase.
- **Comments and docstrings:** This is useful data, since it helps GitHub Copilot better understand the application.

Model Processing

The next step in the code completion process is where the prompt is sent to the LLM. However, there is some latency since the information is sent via the cloud. There is also the time needed to process the prompt.

FIGURE 4.1   The data flow process for code completion in GitHub Copilot.

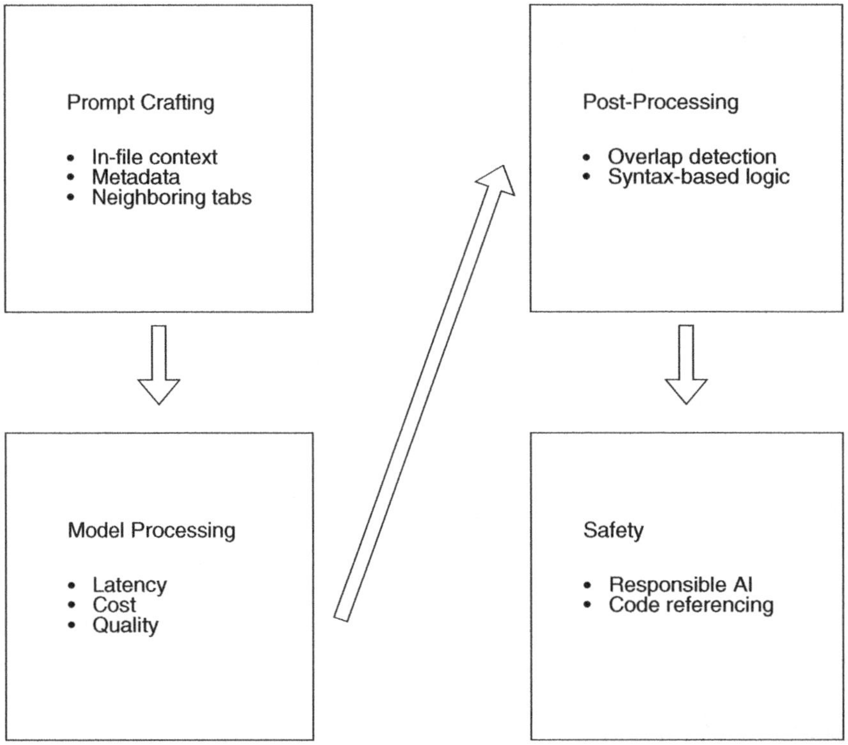

This can be an issue for a programmer who wants to remain in the flow of development. Even a small delay can be frustrating.

Because of this, GitHub Copilot needs to make tradeoffs with the latency and quality of code created. What to do? First, it will give priority to analyzing the active file's content. This is typically the most important area when changes are being made. After this, there's an emphasis on relevant code snippets from open tabs.

But GitHub has other techniques to improve latency. One is advanced datacenter optimization, which is where prompts are routed closer datacenters.

Another approach is to try to understand when there is a need for faster responses. For this, GitHub Copilot will interrupt the typical process and likely render minimal code.

Post-Processing

After GitHub Copilot has generated a response, there may need to be adjustments and refinements. These can be for details like alignment of indention, handling of overlapping code—such as for redundant parentheses or backets—and other formatting. These actions can mitigate syntax errors.

Safety

In the final stage of GitHub Copilot's code completion process, a safety filter is applied to the generated code. This is to evaluate the code for responsible AI practices and basic security precautions. There is also code referencing, which you learned about in Chapter 3.

Note that GitHub Copilot Chat also uses the four-step process for code completion. But there is an important difference: there is generally more time allocated for responses in Chat. The main reason is that there are usually more complicated coding tasks, debugging, unit tests, and explanations. For these, developers are usually more patient since they generally prefer more comprehensive responses.

The GitHub Copilot Trust Center is a helpful resource that provides comprehensive details about the platform's security, privacy, compliance, and intellectual property practices. You can visit it at `https://copilot.github.trust.page/`.

Limitations of GitHub Copilot When Using Data

This book so far has covered many limitations of GitHub Copilot and LLMs. Generally, they are about the underlying datasets used to train the models. Even though GitHub Copilot uses enormous amounts of data, there are still many gaps. It's typical that there are sparse amounts of training data for legacy languages like Fortran and COBOL. At the same time, there may be little or no data on new frameworks or libraries. The reason is that the models are pretrained as of a certain date.

Another issue is with the context window of the LLM, which is the amount of text that it can process at once (covered in Chapter 1). The problem is that a codebase—at least for a production-grade application—is often larger. This means that the LLM will not have a full understanding of the relationships and connections.

For example, suppose you are working on a sophisticated ecommerce application that has over 100,000 lines of code. It has many modules that are dependent on each other, such as for authentication, inventory management, product catalogs, shopping carts, and order processing.

If you use GitHub Copilot to suggest changes to the code for order processing, it is likely not to be as effective if the LLM does not have a full grasp of how this impacts inventory management. In some cases, the code may not work or may even have security vulnerabilities.

It's true that context windows are getting larger. But size is not the only important factor. The LLM may still generate low-quality or false responses because of the difficulties in processing the large amounts of data.

However, there are other limitations of GitHub Copilot and LLMs to consider. For example, the frequency of code patterns in the training dataset can have a major impact on the suggestions. What this means is that the systems will generally adopt standard or common coding practices. Or it may even reflect poor coding practices, assuming they are common.

The LLMs may be skewed too. This can mean that the LLM will focus more on popular frameworks. Yet there may be others that would offer a better solution for a coding task.

Another impact is that the LLM will be mostly about traditional approaches. In other words, the responses may not be as innovative or unconventional.

Reasoning and Context vs. Calculations

When it comes to GitHub Copilot and LLMs, it is usually most effective when it comes to reasoning and context-based tasks. These systems will leverage content—such as the existing codebase and file structure—to get an understanding of the problem. A key to this is how the user crafts a prompt.

Where AI coding systems often fall short, though, is with mathematical calculations. Even with simple math, the results can be off base. Why is this the case? The reason is the underlying transformer model. If a math problem is not represented adequately in the training data, then there will likely be an incorrect response. Keep in mind that GitHub Copilot and LLMs do not have math engines.

Summary

This chapter explained how GitHub Copilot and LLMs work with data. This included an overview of the drivers for the growth of data. It also looked at the challenges with using LLMs for software development, such as with the limited context windows and the issues with data scarcity.

After this, the chapter covered the data flows in GitHub Copilot and LLMs. There are four major steps for how this is done when managing the processing of commands from users: prompt crafting, model processing, post-processing, and safety.

The chapter closed by evaluating the limitations of data workflows with GitHub Copilot and LLMs.

The next chapter covers prompt crafting and prompt engineering.

Exam Essentials

Understand the data security features of GitHub Copilot.   A key benefit is that the tool is hosted on Azure. GitHub Copilot also secures data with encryption, for data in rest, in transit, and in use. There is even an AI-powered vulnerability prevention system to block insecure code. Another layer of security is a proxy filter, which blocks unwanted content.

Know about how GitHub Copilot Individual handles data.   For your prompts, the system will transmit them to GitHub's servers for processing the response. But after this, the data is discarded. GitHub Copilot does not use this information for training its own LLMs.

Understand the data flow of GitHub Copilot.   There are four steps: prompt crafting, model processing, post-processing, and safety. These are for code completions and for Chat. However, in the case of Chat, the system will take longer to process a response. This is because users expect a more comprehensive explanation.

Learn about the limitations of GitHub Copilot when using data.   Be sure to know about how the context window can lead to less effective results. You should also understand the potential impact of the underlying dataset. This may lead to results that focus mostly on traditional approaches to software development and may not be as innovative. Then there is the impact of the cut-off data of a model, which can mean getting old software methods.

Understand reasoning and context versus calculations.   GitHub Copilot is usually better at handling tasks that require reasoning and context. However, it tends to fall short when doing strict mathematical calculations. The reason is the transformer model, which does not have a math engine.

Review Questions

1. What happens to user input data in GitHub Copilot Individual?

    A. It is stored indefinitely for future model training.

    B. It is shared with vetted third-party developers for feedback.

    C. It is processed in real-time but not stored permanently.

    D. It is encrypted but retrievable by the user.

2. What is the role of GitHub Copilot's proxy service?

    A. To run code in the IDE

    B. To filter sensitive data before sending it to the AI model

    C. To increase the speed of code suggestions

    D. To store previous user inputs for reference

3. What factor impacts the relevance of GitHub Copilot's code suggestions?

    A. The recency and frequency of training data examples

    B. The number of developers using GitHub Copilot

    C. The geographic location of the user

    D. The amount of storage available in the user's IDE

4. What security feature does GitHub Copilot provide to detect potential IP violations?

    A. It references generated code against a database of public repositories.

    B. It checks code completions against court opinions.

    C. It discards all long suggestions after they are generated.

    D. It blocks code completions containing certain keywords.

5. What is a key difference in processing between GitHub Copilot's code completion and the Chat feature?

    A. Chat responses generally take longer as they require more comprehensive analysis.

    B. Code completion processes only numerical data, while Chat handles text-based queries.

    C. Chat generates responses automatically, while code completion requires user confirmation.

    D. Code completion is always slower than Chat.

6. How does GitHub Copilot handle prompts to improve the accuracy of code suggestions?

    A. It randomly selects previous suggestions from other users.

    B. It scans the entire project repository for related code.

    C. It retrieves previous AI-generated suggestions stored in a database.

    D. It builds prompts by analyzing the code context, comments, and cursor position.

7. What is a key limitation of GitHub Copilot when performing calculations?

    A. It prioritizes mathematical operations over code completions.

    B. It prevents users from writing mathematical functions.

    C. It lacks a dedicated math engine and relies on training data for numerical reasoning.

    D. It automatically executes calculations before generating code.

8. What impact does the age of an AI model's training data have on its performance?

    A. Older training data may lead to outdated or less relevant suggestions.

    B. AI models always update their training data automatically.

    C. Older training data is always more reliable than new data.

    D. The age of training data has no effect on model accuracy.

9. Why does GitHub Copilot not store user input permanently?

    A. Because storing data permanently is too expensive

    B. Because GitHub does not use any AI models

    C. To protect user privacy

    D. Because it does not have the capability to process real-time inputs

10. What happens if GitHub Copilot identifies code that matches publicly available code?

    A. It alerts the user and provides details on the matched code and its license.

    B. It automatically deletes the suggestion and does not notify the user.

    C. It replaces the code with a generic placeholder.

    D. It allows the user to continue using the suggestion without notification.

11. What is a key advantage of GitHub Copilot Chat over traditional code completion?

    A. It can automatically apply changes to an entire repository.

    B. It operates without any cloud-based processing.

    C. It is designed specifically for hardware programming.

    D. It can generate more comprehensive and context-aware explanations.

12. What is a key limitation of GitHub Copilot when analyzing large codebases?

    A. It scans the entire repository before generating suggestions.

    B. It requires users to manually submit queries for every suggestion.

    C. It can only process a limited amount of surrounding code at a time.

    D. It cannot work with modern programming languages.

13. What is an important step in GitHub Copilot's post-processing stage?

    A. Formatting the generated code to align with proper indentation and syntax

    B. Automatically executing the code to check for errors

    C. Sending suggestions to other developers for peer review

    D. Encrypting all suggestions before displaying them to users

14. What happens if a developer is using GitHub Copilot in an air-gapped environment?

   A. GitHub Copilot will store all user inputs locally for later processing.

   B. GitHub Copilot will not function since it requires an active Internet connection.

   C. GitHub Copilot will process requests using offline models.

   D. GitHub Copilot will require manual approval for each generated suggestion.

15. What is a key reason why AI models require high-quality data for training?

   A. To ensure that AI-generated content is more creative than human-written content

   B. To reduce biases and improve the accuracy of model predictions

   C. To allow AI models to generate unlimited amounts of synthetic data without human input

   D. To increase the speed at which AI models process user requests

16. Why does GitHub Copilot prioritize analyzing the active file's content when generating suggestions?

   A. To ensure that suggestions remain relevant to the user's current coding task

   B. To prevent users from switching between multiple files

   C. To limit the number of suggestions Copilot provides

   D. To store the entire project's data for future suggestions

17. What happens if a GitHub Copilot user disables telemetry data collection?

   A. Copilot will stop generating any code suggestions.

   B. The user's usage data will no longer be collected for analytics and improvements.

   C. The user will lose access to all Copilot features.

   D. The user's code will be shared publicly instead.

18. What role does metadata play in GitHub Copilot's code suggestions?

   A. It automatically saves user-generated code for future reuse.

   B. It determines whether a user is allowed to use Copilot.

   C. It prevents Copilot from generating suggestions for certain programming languages.

   D. It helps provide context for more relevant and accurate completions.

19. What is a key security concern when using AI-powered coding assistants like GitHub Copilot?

   A. AI-generated code may unintentionally include vulnerabilities like hard-coded credentials.

   B. AI will eventually replace all human programmers.

   C. AI-generated code is always more secure than human-written code.

   D. AI models require users to submit their personal information.

20. What is one way GitHub Copilot optimizes performance for developers?

    A. By limiting the number of code suggestions per day

    B. By requiring manual approval for every suggestion

    C. By forcing users to manually enter their code for processing

    D. By prioritizing low-latency response times through cloud infrastructure

Notes

1. Rivery Blog (December 2024). Big Data Statistics: How Much Data Is There in the World? https://rivery.io/blog/big-data-statistics-how-much-data-is-there-in-the-world (accessed 26 February 2025).
2. Edge Delta Blog (March 2024). Breaking Down the Numbers: How Much Data Does The World Create Daily in 2024? https://edgedelta.com/company/blog/how-much-data-is-created-per-day (accessed 26 February 2025).
3. Statista (October 2024). Mobile Data Traffic Per Smartphone Worldwide from 2016 to 2029 (in GB/Month). https://www.statista.com/statistics/738977/worldwide-monthly-data-traffic-per-smartphone/ (accessed 26 February 2025).
4. Global Insights Blog (February 2025). Global Social Media Statistics Research Summary. https://www.smartinsights.com/social-media-marketing/social-media-strategy/new-global-social-media-research/ (accessed 26 February 2025).
5. Bernard Marr & Co. Blog. How Much Data Do We Create Every Day? The Mind-Blowing Stats Everyone Should Read. https://bernardmarr.com/how-much-data-do-we-create-every-day-the-mind-blowing-stats-everyone-should-read/ (accessed 26 February 2025).
6. Demandsage Blog (December 2024). 27 Video Marketing Statistics 2025 — New Data & Trends. https://www.demandsage.com/video-marketing-statistics (accessed 26 February 2025).
7. The Living Library Blog (August 2023). Experts: 90% of Online Content Will Be AI-Generated by 2026. https://thelivinglib.org/experts-90-of-online-content-will-be-ai-generated-by-2026/ (accessed 26 February 2025).
8. Aro Blog (April 2023). IoT Devices "to Generate Nearly 80 Zettabytes of Data" by 2025. https://aro.tech/insights/blog/iot-devices-to-generate-nearly-80-zettabytes-of-data-by-2025/ (accessed 26 February 2025).
9. *The Wall Street Journal* (February 2025). Tech Giants Double Down on Their Massive AI Spending. https://www.wsj.com/tech/ai/tech-giants-double-down-on-their-massive-ai-spending-b3040b33 (accessed 26 February 2025).
10. U.S. Department of Energy (December 2024). DOE Releases New Report Evaluating Increase in Electricity Demand from Data Centers. https://www.energy.gov/articles/doe-releases-new-report-evaluating-increase-electricity-demand-data-centers (accessed 26 February 2025).
11. *The Wall Street Journal* (October 2024). Nuclear-Powered AI: Big Tech's Bold Solution or a Pipedream?. https://www.wsj.com/business/energy-oil/nuclear-power-artificial-intelligence-tech-bb673012 (accessed 26 February 2025).
12. Meta Blog (April 2024). Introducing Meta Llama 3: The Most Capable Openly Available LLM to Date. https://ai.meta.com/blog/meta-llama-3/ (accessed 26 February 2025).

13. Observer (July 2024). A.I. Companies Are Running Out of Training Data: Study. https://observer.com/2024/07/ai-training-data-crisis/ (accessed 26 February 2025).

14. *The Wall Street Journal* (December 2024). The Next Great Leap in AI Is Behind Schedule and Crazy Expensive. https://www.wsj.com/tech/ai/openai-gpt5-orion-delays-639e7693 (accessed 26 February 2025).

15. https://openai.com/charter

16. TechTarget (January 2025). 35 Cybersecurity Statistics to Lose Sleep Over in 2025. https://www.techtarget.com/whatis/34-Cybersecurity-Statistics-to-Lose-Sleep-Over-in-2020 (accessed 26 February 2025).

17. IBM (2024). Cost of a Data Breach Report 2024. https://www.ibm.com/reports/data-breach (accessed 26 February 2025).

Chapter

5

Prompt Crafting and Engineering

THE GITHUB COPILOT EXAM OBJECTIVES COVERED IN THIS CHAPTER INCLUDE, BUT ARE NOT LIMITED TO, THE FOLLOWING:

✔ **Domain 4: Prompt Crafting and Prompt Engineering**

- Describe the fundamentals of prompt crafting

  - Describe how the context for the prompt is determined

  - Describe the language options for promoting GitHub Copilot

  - Describe the different parts of a prompt

  - Describe the role of prompting

  - Describe the difference between zero-shot and few-shot prompting

  - Describe the way chat history is used with GitHub Copilot

  - Identify prompt crafting best practices when using GitHub Copilot

- Describe the fundamentals of prompt engineering

  - Explain prompt engineering principles, training methods, and best practices

  - Describe the prompt process flow

The GitHub Copilot certification study guide mentions both prompt crafting and prompt engineering. What do these mean? Aren't they essentially the same?

Well, interestingly enough, they are! Both describe how to put together clear and specific prompts to get the responses you want. This chapter refers to these together as prompt engineering—just to make things simpler.

Understanding this skill is certainly important because it goes to the heart of working with GitHub Copilot. Of course, it's also a key part of the certification exam. This chapter covers what you need to know.

We'll start by describing how AI coding requires a different mindset. Yes, it's often about coming up with the right prompt. Next, we look at the issues with prompt engineering, as it is far from a perfect science.

After this, the chapter covers the structure of a typical prompt, which includes four parts. They include context, instructions for the LLMs, input of the content, and format for the responses. You'll look at examples of each of these steps.

You will then look at best practices for prompt engineering, which is the most extensive part of the chapter. This highlights the importance of this topic for the exam.

The chapter ends by covering other details about GitHub Copilot, such as language support. There are also some predictions about how prompt engineering will change in the future.

Mastering the art of prompt engineering is essential for effectively using AI systems like GitHub Copilot. This skill involves creating precise and well-structured instructions to ensure the generated code meets the specific needs of your project. The quality of the AI's output is closely tied to the clarity and specificity of your prompts.

Different Mindset

Prompt engineering is a fairly new field. It emerged in 2018 when the first LLMs, like GPT-2, came onto the scene. AI researchers began to study how to best use these systems, which was often about developing effective prompts.

But of course, prompt engineering would not become part of the mainstream until 2022, which is when OpenAI launched ChatGPT. Suddenly, millions were prompting this application. Not long after this, prompt engineering would become a skillset for various jobs.

Prompt engineering is essentially a blend of creativity and technical ability. In terms of creativity, it is about using the right words, tone, and phrasing to nudge the LLM into a particular direction. This means you need a good grasp of the language and an understanding of nuance.

This can be challenging for developers since writing code is about understanding structure and logic. True, there is some creativity involved. A coding problem often has many different approaches. But for the most part, applications are predictable, with loops, conditions, and variables. It's like a complex math problem.

At the same time, prompt engineering does have some analytical characteristics. A good prompt should be precise and consistent.

Despite all this, many software developers are able to make the transition. There is no need to take expensive courses either. The general principles are actually straightforward.

Ultimately, it will mean a different mindset and approach to traditional programming. As you learned in Chapter 1, you will usually start a task not by writing code, but with a prompt. Then you will analyze the generated code—and may have to use more prompts to refine it. It can seem somewhat convoluted, but this approach to programming has been shown to be faster and to improve code quality.

Issues with Prompt Engineering

Sometimes prompt engineering can be frustrating. It may take numerous iterations to get a good response, which can be time-consuming. In some cases, you may not get anything that works right.

This is due to the inherent issues with LLMs. These models are based on complex probabilities of the transformer model, which are grounded in massive datasets. But the models may sometimes make the wrong predictions because they are not detecting the correct patterns or the underlying data may be too sparse or even wrong.

Here are some of the other problems with prompt engineering:

- **Model differences:** Even if you are not having problems with a model, there can still be inconsistent results. For example, Google's Gemini may generate different code or provide other explanations when compared to, say, Anthropic's Claude or OpenAI's o1. Each has their own proprietary algorithms. As you saw in Chapter 2, these models can be difficult to evaluate.

- **Prompt length:** A verbose prompt can cause the LLM to misinterpret or overlook important details. It's known as getting "lost in the middle." This is why it's generally a good idea to focus on one task at a time.

- **Formatting:** LLMs can generate output in certain formats, like JSON. But the results can sometimes be inconsistent or incorrect. Because of this, you usually need to be more specific with your prompt. An example of a prompt is *Generate a JSON object with the following format.* Then you would provide an example of what you are looking for.

Fundamentals of Prompt Engineering

There are no magical shortcuts to prompt engineering. It's mostly about applying a few principles and dedicating time to practice and experimentation. If you look at guidelines published from providers like OpenAI, you'll notice that they are not long.

However, the field of prompt engineering is not static either. It evolves as the underlying models do. Changes can mean that a prompt you have relied on suddenly stops working the way you want it to.

But the good news is that there are some fundamentals that are likely to be reliable for prompt engineering. You also need to know about them for the exam. The next few sections look at these fundamentals.

Prompt Structure

Again, there are no clear-cut rules for prompt engineering. But Figure 5.1 shows a four-step approach that covers the fundamentals. GitHub refers to this as the primary, supporting, and grounding of the content for the prompt.

You do not need to have all four elements in a prompt. It depends on the use case. Sometimes a simple prompt is fine. Let's take a look at the components of a prompt.

FIGURE 5.1   Key elements of a prompt structure.

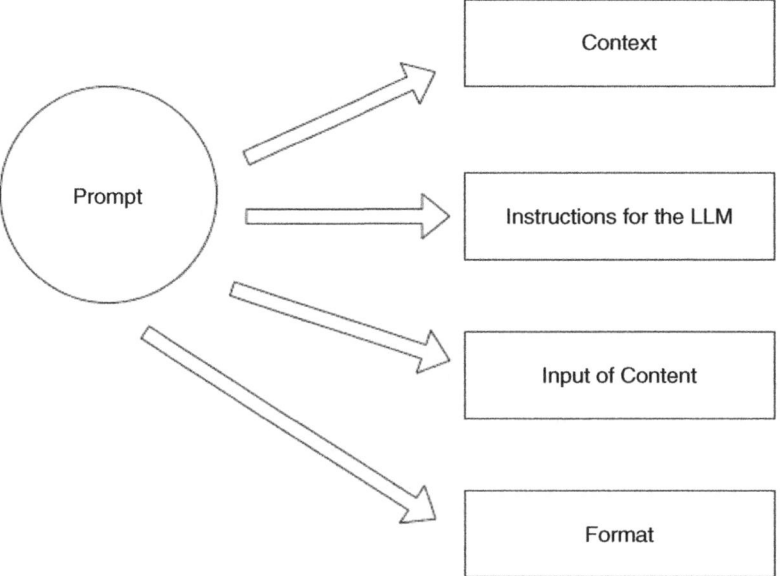

Context

Context refers to the initial information or setting provided within a prompt, which helps guide the LLM's response. This often involves assigning a specific role or persona to the AI. This helps tailor its output to be more relevant and accurate.

Typically, a prompt begins with a brief statement that establishes this context. For example, if you want help with debugging Python code, you might start with:

> *I'm a Python developer experienced in debugging complex scripts.*

Or to obtain guidance on optimizing SQL queries, you could begin with:

> *I'm a database administrator skilled in SQL query optimization.*

By clearly defining the context, you enable the LLM to approach your query with the appropriate perspective. This is also the initial step of GitHub Copilot's data flow, which you learned about in Chapter 4. It's about analyzing the current file, cursor position, and recent edits to prepare a prompt to be processed by the LLM.

This also includes details from the chat history. By understanding the flow of the conversion, this will allow for more relevant responses from the LLM. The chat history may also reveal the user's preferences, which can help with personalization. For example, if you are chatting about Python functions, then the responses will reflect the approach and conventions for this language.

Instructions for the LLM

When putting a prompt together for GitHub Copilot, you'll need at least one clear instruction. If not, the LLM will not know what to do. It will probably say something like, "Sorry, I can't assist with that."

An instruction is often straightforward. It can be something like to create or debug code.

You are certainly not limited to one instruction either. But you need to be careful. The LLM may prioritize one of the instructions over another and sometimes there may be confusion of what needs to be done. After all, an LLM can't read your mind!

The bottom line: A single, well-defined instruction per prompt usually gets the best results.

In this book so far, you have looked at a myriad of instructions. But there are many more. For example, a powerful feature for an LLM is summarization. These systems are particularly good at processing large amounts of information and getting to the heart of the matter. Summarization can be a huge time saver.

Here are some example scenarios:

- **Bug reports:** You can pinpoint the main issues for users. Here's a sample prompt: *Summarize the key problems mentioned in these bug reports to identify the critical issues needing attention.*

■ **Change logs:** The LLM can quickly grasp the major updates in a new software version. Here's a sample prompt: *Summarize the major changes highlighted in the version 2.0 release notes.*

■ **Documentation:** True, you can use a search to find pertinent information. But this could still miss the gist of what you are looking for. But with an LLM, you can create a brief summary of the core functions, dependencies, and structures. A sample prompt is as follows: *Provide a concise summary of the following documentation, emphasizing the main features and codebase structure.*

■ **Research papers:** With the growth in AI, there has been a proliferation of research papers. You can find many of them on sites like arXiv, which is at `https://arxiv.org/`. Using summarization, you can easily extract key insights and even compare these to other papers. Here's an example prompt: *Summarize the main findings and innovations discussed in this research paper.* For state-of-the-art LLMs, the research and summarization capabilities are getting much better, such as with ChatGPT's powerful Deep research feature.

■ **Email threads:** Keeping track of these can be challenging. But this is not the case with LLMs. You can capture the essence of lengthy email discussions. Here's an example prompt: *Summarize the key points and decisions from the following email conversation.*

Foreign language translation is another area where LLMs are quite useful, as these systems are effective in understanding the intricate patterns of languages. In fact, this can be helpful for localization of software applications. Here are some examples:

■ **UI element translation:** You can translate the words for common elements like buttons, menus, and dialog boxes. Here's a sample prompt: *Convert the following button labels into Spanish: Start, Cancel, Settings and Log Out.*

■ **Tooltip translation:** This is where you have a brief description of a function, such as for the UI. Here is an example prompt: *Translate the following tooltips into Korean: "Drag to move this item, Click to add a new contact, Double-click to view details."*

However, as with anything generated from an LLM, you need to review the responses. Sometimes the system can get things wrong. With language translation, the LLM may miss the idiomatic expressions, cultural nuances, or subtle meanings unique to a particular context. Making a mistake can have major consequences because you might offend or confuse users.

To help create effective prompts, there are *prompt libraries*, which are curated collections of prompts. They can be good starting points. They can also spark ideas. An example of a prompt library—located at `https://github.com/aymalkhalid/AI-Prompt-Library-for-Software-Development`—is from Aymal Khalid Khan, a software developer. Another useful one is for the Cursor AI coding tool and is located at `https://cursor.directory/`. You can use the prompts for GitHub Copilot as well.

Input of Content

It can be helpful to add some structure to your prompts. A common method is to use ### or quotation marks. This helps the LLM better distinguish between the instructions and the content you want it to process.

Take a look at an example. Suppose you want to summarize the key steps of a comprehensive document about a new API that you want to use for your application.

Here's a way to structure a prompt:

> *Extract the main steps for implementing the API from the content provided below:*
> ###
> *{Insert API documentation here}*
> ###

With this prompt, the LLM will have a clearer focus and you should get a better response.

Format

With your prompt, you can specify how the LLM should format the output. This can be helpful in certain areas, such as when you need something in JSON or another structure.

This is a sample prompt:

> *Create a Python function that accepts a list of dictionaries, each representing an employee with their employee_id and department. The function should return a JSON object that groups employees by their departments. Format the output to include both the function and an example usage with sample input and output.*

This is the output:

```
{
  "code": "def group_employees_by_department(employees):\n    department_
map = {}\n    for employee in employees:\n        department =
employee['department']\n        if department not in department_map:\n
        department_map[department] = []\n        department_map
[department].append(employee['employee_id'])\n    return department_map",
  "example_usage": {
    "input": [
      {"employee_id": 101, "department": "HR"},
      {"employee_id": 102, "department": "IT"},
      {"employee_id": 103, "department": "HR"},
      {"employee_id": 104, "department": "IT"},
      {"employee_id": 105, "department": "Finance"}
    ],
    "output": {
      "HR": [101, 103],
      "IT": [102, 104],
      "Finance": [105]
    }
  }
}
}
```

Best Practices

This section looks at the best practices for prompt engineering. It's important to keep in mind that there are no strict rules. Rather, these are flexible guidelines. They have nuances and may also evolve as LLMs change. But as you work more with these systems, you will pick up your own approaches. A key to prompt engineering is experimentation.

Be Clear

The best practice of "be clear" is perhaps the most important one for prompt engineering. The LLM needs to have enough context to understand what you really want. Often, this means being specific and spelling things out. This should help reduce inaccuracies and hallucinations.

A good way to get a sense of this best practice is to consider some examples—that is, a comparison of vague and clear prompts:

> **Original prompt:** *Write a script for authentication.*
> **Better prompt:** *Build a Python script using Flask that implements user authentication. Include routes for user registration, login, and logout. Store user data in an SQLite database, hashing passwords securely using the bcrypt library.*
> **Original prompt:** *Write a function to sort data.*
> **Better prompt:** *Write a Python function called sort_numbers that takes a list of integers as input and returns the list sorted in ascending order. Include an optional parameter to sort in descending order if specified.*
> **Original prompt:** *Generate a web scraper.*
> **Better prompt:** *Write a Python script using the BeautifulSoup library to scrape job postings from a specified web page. Extract the job title, company name, location, and job description, and save the results in a CSV file.*

Another helpful best practice is to write out acronyms and define technical terms. No doubt, the world of software development is filled with plenty of jargon. But sometimes it can be confusing for LLMs to understand and differentiate the terminology.

> Here's a prompt:
>
> *CI build failing. How to fix it?*

This lacks enough detail. The phrase "CI build failing" could refer to numerous issues like dependency errors, misconfigured pipelines, or network problems.

> A better version is the following:
>
> *My Jenkins CI pipeline is failing during the Build stage with an error: "Maven dependency not found: org.apache.maven.plugins:maven-compiler-plugin:3.8.1'." How can I resolve this?*

This prompt is much clearer. It specifies the CI tool (Jenkins), the failing stage (Build), the specific error message (Maven dependency not found), and the context (Maven plugin version). This level of technical detail ensures that the LLM has enough information to provide actionable advice.

TABLE 5.1   Leading Words

Context	Leading Word
C function declaration	`Int`
JavaScript promise	`Promise`
HTML image element	`<img`
SQL query for creating a table	`CREATE TABLE`

Leading Words

For prompt engineering, the concept of "leading words" is about using terms or phrases to nudge the LLM to generate certain types of responses. Think of this as about a cue. In fact, "leading words" can be one word.

So how does this help? Consider an example.

Suppose that your code has this comment:

```
# A Python class called 'Employee' with fields for name, ID, and position.
```

Then, when you enter `class`, GitHub will understand what you are referring to. It's to create the `Employee` class. The code will be generated, and you can accept or reject it.

Table 5.1 shows some other examples of leading words and how they can impact a model's output.

Leading Questions

Popular court TV shows often have attorneys who ask dramatic leading questions, like "You saw the defendant at the scene of the crime, didn't you?" They are a way to suggest an answer, so as to sway the jury. But when an attorney asks a leading question for their own witnesses, they are not allowed. They are too prejudicial.

When it comes to prompt engineering, a similar dynamic is at work. A leading question can often result in a response that is skewed. Part of this is due to the fact that LLMs are designed to be helpful with their response. But this can mean that they will try to reinforce the user's assumptions.

Here's an example of a prompt that's a leading question:

Isn't using recursion always better than iteration in programming because it's more efficient?

A more neutral and balanced approach would be:

What are the advantages and disadvantages of using recursion compared to iteration in programming?

By taking a neutral approach, you are guiding the LLM to provide more comprehensive and balanced responses.

Use Analogies or Comparisons

If you are unfamiliar with a programming concept and want a more understandable explanation of it, you can ask for an analogy with your prompt. For example, suppose you do not know how recursion works. You can use this prompt:

Describe recursion using an analogy.

GitHub provides a response that compares this programming technique to nested Russian dolls, with each level of recursion representing a different doll. This is certainly a good response. It effectively explains a complex topic in a clear and relatable way.

Ask for Alternatives

A good way to help solve a problem is to explore alternatives. You can get a better understanding of the different approaches and their tradeoffs.

For instance, instead of simply requesting a basic solution, such as with this prompt:

Create a function to sort a list.

You could take it a step further by asking:

Write two functions to sort a list—one that uses Python's built-in sorted() method and another that implements the bubble sort algorithm. Compare their efficiency.

To help further your understanding, you might then ask:

What are the advantages and disadvantages of each method?

Zero- and Few-Shot Learning

Zero-shot learning is how we typically interact with GitHub Copilot, in which a prompt will not have any examples. Rather, you rely on the pre-trained knowledge of the LLM for the response.

Here is an example:

Write a Python function to calculate the factorial of a given number using recursion.

Often, zero-shot learning works fine. But sometimes you need something more sophisticated, and this is where *few-shot learning* comes in. This is where you provide some examples in your prompt. These examples provide context for the LLM to understand a task's structure and requirements.

For example, suppose you want to create a function that generates the numbers with a range. You can use this prompt:

Based on the following examples of:
Input: start=1, end=10
Output: [2, 3, 5, 7]

Input: start=11, end=20
Output: [11, 13, 17, 19]

Input: start=21, end=30
Output: [23, 29]

Generate a Python function that takes a start and end range as input and returns a list of prime numbers within that range.

You start with a few examples and then follow this up with an instruction. This should provide a better response than a generic prompt.

Chain-of-Thought (CoT) Prompting

Chain-of-thought (CoT) prompting is a way to help improve the problem-solving capabilities of an LLM. It's about breaking down complex problems into logical and easier steps. For each of these, there is a process that focuses on explaining the reasoning. The result is likely to be more accurate responses.

However, CoT prompting can be tricky. The prompts need to be well thought-out.

CoT prompting can be particularly useful for software development. It can help with tasks that often involve multiple steps, such as debugging and algorithm design.

Table 5.2 shows an example.

Mitigating Hallucinations

In Chapter 2, you learned that one of the biggest drawbacks of LLMs is that they can sometimes generate *hallucinations*. This is when the response contains false or misleading information. This issue is especially problematic in software development, where precision and correctness are critical.

The good news is that there are prompting strategies that can mitigate this issue:

- **Request specific responses:** In the prompt, specify what you want the response to be. This helps the LLM understand the boundaries. Here's a prompt: *Is the following SQL query syntax correct? Provide a "yes" or "no" response and briefly explain why this is the case.*

- **Provide choices:** Limit the response to a fixed number of options. Here is a sample prompt: *Which of the following is a valid technique to debug JavaScript: using console. log, running a debugger, or rewriting the code in Python?*

- **Request the reasoning:** Ask the LLM to justify the response, which can help reveal potential errors or gaps in the reasoning. Here is a prompt: *Provide a step-by-step explanation why the following Python function generates a syntax error. Then correct the error.*

Another way to deal with hallucinations is to follow a best practice mentioned earlier in the chapter: be clear. This is perhaps the best approach.

TABLE 5.2   Example of CoT Prompting

Step in the Process	Prompt
Understand the requirement	*I need to create a REST API for a task management system using Node.js and Express. The API should allow users to create, read, update, and delete tasks. Where should I start?*
Set up the environment	*Let's begin by setting up a Node.js project. How can I initialize the project and set up Express?*
Create the task model	*Now that Express is set up, I need to define a task model for the system. How should I structure this model?*
Implement the Create endpoint	*How can I implement an endpoint to create a new task, ensuring that required fields are validated?*
Implement the Read endpoint	*How can I implement an endpoint to create a new task, ensuring that required fields are validated?*
Implement the Update endpoint	*How should I create an endpoint to update an existing task, ensuring that only valid fields are updated?*
Implement the Delete endpoint	*Finally, how can I implement an endpoint to delete a task by its ID, ensuring that it's removed from the database?*

Security and Privacy

When you write prompts, you should always be mindful of potential security and privacy issues. In some cases, you may be working with *personally identifiable information (PII)*. This is data that can identify a person, such as with an address, social security number, email, or phone number. Generally, this is information that should be protected and secured.

These are the kinds of prompts you should avoid:

How would you investigate a billing discrepancy reported by Michael Johnson, account number 123456789?

Instead, you should generalize the prompt:

How would you investigate a billing discrepancy reported by a customer?

This revision protects sensitive information while still providing the context needed to address the issue.

Multimodal Systems

A *multimodal* system is an LLM that integrates different forms of content creation, such as text, sound, images, and video. For example, with ChatGPT you can use DALL-E for image generation. Here's a prompt:

> *Create an image of a dense fog rolling through a mystical pine forest, with rays of sunlight piercing through the canopy.*

Figure 5.2 shows the resulting image.

With DALL-E, you can also upload an image and the system will interpret it. This can be useful for analyzing mockups or reference images. ChatGPT can then generate the code for it.

However, GitHub Copilot is not multimodal. Rather, you need to use the Vision for Copilot Preview extension, which is located at `https://github.com/microsoft/vscode-copilot-vision/blob/main/README.md`. This allows you to add images to Chat by dragging them in or pasting them from the clipboard. There is API integration with OpenAI, Azure OpenAI, Anthropic, and Gemini. You need to create accounts for these to get access to the API keys.

GitHub has plans to have a built-in image feature, so the extension is likely a temporary solution.

FIGURE 5.2   Image created by DALL-E.

Generated with AI using DALL·E - OpenAI

Language Support

When you write a prompt in GitHub Copilot, you usually do not have to specify the programming language. The system will understand what you want based on the code file you are working on.

Of course, sometimes you may want to use another programming language. Then which ones does GitHub Copilot support? There is no list. But the number is likely to be large, as the system's dataset includes the repositories of GitHub and other sources across the Internet. According to analysis from DistantJob, there are about 265 programming languages in existence.[1]

But the quality of the code generation can vary when using GitHub Copilot, especially for obscure languages. This is why its customization features are so important.

The Future of Prompt Engineering

Having to craft prompts seems kind of backwards. If AI is truly intelligent, why should users need to put so much effort into this process?

This is certainly a legitimate concern. Some say that prompt engineering is not a feature, but a bug!

In the years ahead, the use of prompt engineering is likely to fade in usage. A major reason for this is the emergence of *agentic AI*. Think of this as the next generation of generative AI. It uses multiple LLMs to engage in planning, reasoning, and tool use to solve complex, multi-step problems. An agentic system will do this autonomously—that is, with no or little human intervention.

The major LLM developers, like OpenAI, Google, and Anthropic, have been aggressively building agentic AI models. In fact, these capabilities are particularly useful for software development, which often involves repetitive tasks and the need for advanced problem solving.

Agentic AI can also allow for collaboration with various agents, known as a multiple-agent system. For example, a project management agent can help draft the requirements, which will then be assigned to a coder agent that will translate them to code. After this, a quality assurance agent will test the application. This can then be returned to the coder for adjustments. This can iterate multiple times—until there is a high-quality application.

If you used a traditional LLM for this, the process would be more time-consuming. You would have to create multiple prompts for each of the steps that the agents handle.

For an agentic system, there will still be some prompting, but the approach will be different from the traditional approaches covered in this chapter. Prompting for an agentic AI system should be short and clear. If you have multiple steps, this can actually hinder the reasoning process.

Summary

This chapter looked at prompt engineering, which is critical for using GitHub Copilot effectively. It began with a look at how this takes a different mindset for developers. The chapter also covered some of the drawbacks of prompt engineering, such as dealing with the differences of AI models and response formats.

You then got an overview of the four main elements of a prompt's structure. They include context, instructions for the LLM, input of the content, and format of the responses.

After this, you learned about the best practices for prompt engineering. Some of the main ones include being clear, asking for alternatives, zero- and few-shot learning, chain-of-thought (CoT) prompting, and methods for mitigating hallucinations.

Finally, you learned about language support for GitHub Copilot and the future of prompt engineering.

The next chapter covers the developer use cases for GitHub Copilot.

Exam Essentials

Know the structure of a prompt. There are four main steps. First, you set the context, such as the role or scenario for the LLM. Next, there are the instructions for the LLM. These are clear tasks to perform. Then there is input for the content. You can add details by using delimiters like ###. Finally, there is the format for the response, such as in JSON.

Learn the best practices for prompt engineering. A prompt should be clear, which helps reduce hallucinations and provide for more relevant responses. You can also use few-shot learning. This is where you provide some examples in the prompt for more context. You can also use chain-of-thought (CoT) prompting, which is about breaking down a task into more understandable parts. This can help LLMs with the problem-solving process. Finally, even when you spend time crafting a prompt, the results can still be off. This is why it's common to iterate.

Understand security with prompting. In some cases, you may work with sensitive data when creating a prompt. You need to make sure you do not disclose this information.

Understand language support. It's not clear how many languages GitHub Copilot supports. But the system certainly can generate code from dozens of languages. However, the quality is dependent on the dataset. For some obscure languages, there may not be enough information to generate useful code.

Review Questions

1. For GitHub Copilot, what is the key reason for prompt engineering?

    A. To change to another large language model

    B. To use multimodal capabilities

    C. To write clear instructions for the large language model to create the best code or response

    D. To automate the SLDC process

2. All of the following are parts of a prompt except the following:

    A. Input of context

    B. Format

    C. Code execution

    D. Context

3. Why is it a good idea to avoid writing long prompts for GitHub Copilot?

    A. They always result in hallucinations.

    B. The large language model may misinterpret or ignore important details.

    C. They will use copyrighted code.

    D. They will generate responses that are too long.

4. In what way does few-shot learning improves the responses of GitHub Copilot?

    A. It includes several examples that help guide the large language model.

    B. It changes the underlying parameters of the large language model.

    C. It increases creativity.

    D. It eliminates mistakes.

5. Why is chain-of-thought (CoT) prompting helpful?

    A. It forces a large language model to answer in either yes or no.

    B. It breaks down complex problems into different steps for improved reasoning.

    C. It increases the speed of the response.

    D. It will mean that the response will use the correct programming language.

6. When writing a prompt for GitHub Copilot, what is a potential security risk?

    A. Using verbose prompts

    B. Asking for XML formatted data

    C. Using the large language model to create data

    D. Including personally identifiable information (PII)

7. Even if you write a clear prompt, why might you still get a false response?

   A. You are using the wrong model.

   B. The model does not have enough relevant data.

   C. You have not adjusted the model.

   D. You did not use a custom model.

8. How is agentic AI likely to change prompt engineering?

   A. The prompts will need to include more details about formatting.

   B. There will be no need for prompts.

   C. The prompts will be shorter.

   D. You will need to rely on prompt libraries.

9. For code generation, which languages does GitHub Copilot support?

   A. The ten most popular languages

   B. Scripting languages like JavaScript and SQL

   C. Only languages created by Microsoft

   D. A wide variety of languages

10. How does zero-shot learning differ from few-shot learning?

   A. Few-shot learning is based on several languages, whereas zero-shot learning is for one language.

   B. Few-shot learning has several examples in a prompt, whereas zero-shot learning has none.

   C. Few-shot learning is for longer code tasks, whereas zero-shot learning is for code snippets.

   D. Few-shot learning is for refactoring code, whereas zero-shot learning is for functions.

11. What is a drawback when using foreign translation with an LLM?

   A. It cannot translate technical jargon.

   B. It may not pick up on idiomatic expressions and cultural nuances.

   C. It cannot work with code.

   D. It only can be used for three languages.

12. Why would you use ### in a prompt?

   A. To separate the instructions from the content

   B. To format responses

   C. To refractor code

   D. To debug code

13. Why would you use leading words in a prompt?

    A. To generate more detailed explanations

    B. To change the format of the response

    C. To encourage a certain type of response

    D. To improve debugging

14. What is a way to reduce hallucinations when writing a prompt?

    A. Write detailed prompts.

    B. Use delimiters.

    C. Use broad language.

    D. Request a clear response, like "Yes" or "No."

15. How does Chat history influence the responses from GitHub Copilot?

    A. They are not used in the processing.

    B. They are used as context to improve the responses.

    C. The instructions are only used for the processing.

    D. This is only used for custom models.

16. Which of the following prompts could be written better?

    A. Code an input form.

    B. `/explain.`

    C. Create a SQL query to list all customers in the database.

    D. Write a Python function that sorts a list of numbers in descending order.

17. What is a disadvantage of chain-of-thought (CoT) prompting?

    A. It can mean less effective debugging.

    B. It cannot be used with the Chat.

    C. It is only available for Python.

    D. It can increase the response time of the LLM.

18. Which of the following may result in less effective responses from GitHub Copilot?

    A. A prompt that is too precise

    B. A prompt with multiple instructions

    C. A prompt that uses some relevant examples

    D. A prompt that uses delimiters

19. Why might you specify a certain role when writing a prompt?

    A. To mitigate creativity of the response

    B. To do code conversion

    C. To provide more context for the LLM

    D. To focus on a certain programming language

20. Why do LLMs like those from OpenAI, Google, and Anthropic generate different responses?

    A. This is based on safety filters.

    B. This is due to human feedback loops.

    C. This is based on the datasets and proprietary algorithms.

    D. The responses are deterministic.

Note

1. DistantJob Blog (September 2024). Programming Languages Ranking: Top 9 in 2024. https://distantjob.com/blog/programming-languages-rank (accessed 27 February 2025).

Chapter

6

Developer Use Cases for GitHub Copilot

THE GITHUB COPILOT EXAM OBJECTIVES COVERED IN THIS CHAPTER INCLUDE, BUT ARE NOT LIMITED TO, THE FOLLOWING:

✔ **Domain 5: Developer use cases for AI**

- Improve developer productivity

  - Describe how AI can improve common use cases for developer productivity

    - Learning new programming languages and frameworks

    - Language translation

    - Context switching

    - Writing documentation

    - Personalized context-aware responses

    - Generating sample data

    - Modernizing legacy applications

    - Debugging code

    - Data science

    - Code refactoring

  - Discuss how GitHub Copilot can help with SDLC (Software Development Life Cycle) management

  - Describe the limitations of using GitHub Copilot

  - Describe how to use the productivity API to see how GitHub Copilot impacts coding

This chapter looks at the developer use cases for GitHub Copilot. There are certainly many available, as there seems to be no end to the capabilities of this powerful tool. But when it comes to the exam, there are certain areas you need to focus on. This is what you'll do in this chapter.

It starts off by looking at how you can use GitHub Copilot as a tool for learning. You can not only learn a new language and framework but also create study guides as well as code challenges for upcoming job interviews.

After this, you learn how GitHub Copilot can generate comments and documentation for your code. Then you look at how you can use this tool with the core capabilities of programming languages, like loops, conditionals, variables, data structures, and functions.

Next, you learn how to use GitHub Copilot to improve the quality of your code. Examples include code refactoring, translation, and debugging techniques.

The chapter even shows how you can use GitHub Copilot to create data, such as for logins. There is then a review of ways to create database schemas like SQL scripts.

The chapter rounds out by explaining how GitHub Copilot can assist with the software development lifecycle (SDLC), as well as using the REST API for evaluating metrics.

Learning

In Chapter 2, you learned about how GitHub Copilot can be an effective tool in learning a new language. This also applies to frameworks, libraries, packages, and dependencies. Often, when code is generated—such as with Chat—there will be an explanation. You can then ask GitHub Copilot about whatever does not make sense.

It's true that there are plenty of resources to help out with the learning process, such as YouTube videos, blogs, bootcamps, books, and so on. When it comes to learning, it's often about what works for you.

But with GitHub Copilot, there are some advantages:

▪ **Personalization:** You can customize the learning with your prompts. For example, you can say something like, "I'm new to Python. How do you use variables?"

- **Tailored code snippets:** A good way to learn is to have GitHub Copilot provide an example. Here's a prompt: "I'm new to JavaScript. Explain how to use conditionals. Provide a simple example."
- **Interactive:** Again, with Chat, you can iterate on certain topics. You can follow up with a prompt when you want to get a better explanation.

The next few sections cover other ways you can use GitHub Copilot as a learning tool.

Learning a Language or Framework

Suppose you want to learn the Go language. You can start with this prompt:

What is the Go language? What are the common use cases? What are the pros and cons?

This will give you a high-level understanding of the language. Then, you can ask GitHub Copilot for next steps in the learning process. Here's a prompt:

What is the best way to start learning Go? Where do I start?

Copilot offers the following options:

- Install Go from the `golang.org` website.
- Set up the environment, such as configuring the workspace and setting up the `GOPATH` environment variable.
- Read the documentation, which is found in the Go Tour section on `golang.org`.
- Learn the basics, like variables, control structures, functions, and error handling.
- Write some programs.
- Learn about the standard library of Go packages. Then build a project.
- Join a community, such as on Slack or Go Forum.
- Learn about the standard library of Go packages.
- Read books and use tutorials. GitHub Copilot provides some recommendations.
- Contribute to the Go open-source project.

All in all, this is a pretty good path for a beginner who wants to get off to a great start with the Go language.

Comparing Languages

When learning a new language, a good approach is to see how it compares to a language you already know. Let's say you have a background in Python, but your new job requires that you learn Rust.

With some prompts in GitHub Copilot, you can tailor your learning. The following are some examples:

I know how to use lists in Python. Can you show me how Rust works with collections, such as vectors?

My background is with Python. So provide an example of a simple Rust function with comments explaining its syntax.

How would you rewrite a Python for-loop in Rust? Please explain. I'm new to Rust.

Please provide a comparison of how Python and Rust work with asynchronous programming.

Study Guides

With GitHub Copilot, you can easily create useful study guides. These can be handy references when you're developing software.

These are some sample prompts:

Write a beginner's study guide for Java. It should have core concepts, examples, and practice questions.

Write a checklist about JavaScript. Make it as practical as possible.

Besides creating study guides for languages, you can focus on a particular topic, such as with these prompts:

Write a simple study guide about object-oriented programming. Focus on key concepts, such as inheritance, polymorphism, and encapsulation. Provide examples.

Write a study guide about version control in Git. Include common commands, such as for cloning, branching, and merging.

Code Challenges

Winston Tang is a veteran developer, having worked at companies like Google and Amazon. In 2015, he founded LeetCode because he saw how many of his friends had difficulty with job interviews. The online platform, which is located at `https://leetcode.com`, provides comprehensive preparation, with thousands of questions. They range from simple problems to advanced puzzles. Just some of the categories include algorithms, system design, and database management. LeetCode also supports a myriad of languages, including Python, Java, C++, and JavaScript.

But interestingly enough, you can use GitHub Copilot to create these types of questions. Here are some sample prompts:

Create a Python coding challenge that is about dynamic programming techniques.

Write a Java coding exercise about finding the shortest path in an unweighted graph.

Besides creating LeetCode questions, you can also have GitHub Copilot solve them. You can have a simple prompt like this:

Below is a LeetCode challenge. Please solve it and explain the steps.

[The LeetCode question].

Documentation

Creating documentation is often one of those tasks that developers dread. If anything, the perception is that well-written code should be self-explanatory. Then there are the trade-offs: Which has more value—creating code or writing documentation? Well, despite all this, documentation is often a critical part of successful software development, and GitHub can assist in the various parts of the process, such as with comments, pull request descriptions, and user guides. A *pull request* is when you merge code changes into the code from one branch to another, which is done in a version control system like GitHub.

Comments

Writing comments in your code can certainly help with the learning process and knowledge sharing. It can mean that your team will not have to spend as much time understanding what you have created.

But writing comments can be tedious. In some cases, they may not necessarily be easy to understand.

Exercise 6.1 shows an example of how you can create comments using GitHub Copilot.

EXERCISE 6.1

Using GitHub Copilot to Create Comments

1. Click the Copilot icon on the top-right side of the screen in VS Code.

2. Select Open Chat.

3. Use this prompt: *Write a function, called* `reverse_string`*, that takes a string as an input and returns the string reversed. Write comments that explain each of the key steps of this program.*

4. The following images shows the response from GitHub Copilot. It inserts comments but also provides a *docstring.* This is used as the first statement in a Python function to describe it.

```
def reverse_string(input_string):
    """
    This function takes a string as input and returns the

    Parameters:
    input_string (str): The string to be reversed.

    Returns:
    str: The reversed string.
    """
    # Step 1: Convert the input string to a list of chara
    char_list = list(input_string)

    # Step 2: Reverse the list of characters
    char list reverse()
```

As AI coding becomes more common, the use of comments may actually start to fade. Why? The reason is that if a developer does not understand a code snippet, they can have the AI coding tool easily provide an explanation.

User Guides

Using GitHub Copilot to write a user guide is similar to the process for creating comments. Exercise 6.2 shows the steps for this.

EXERCISE 6.2

Using GitHub Copilot to Create User Documentation

1. Click the Copilot icon on the top-right side of the screen in VS Code.

2. Select Open Chat.

3. Use this prompt: *Generate API documentation for this REST endpoint. Write this in Markdown format.*

4. The following image shows the response from GitHub Copilot. The API documentation includes details about the endpoints and even provides code examples.

API Documentation

Base URL

```
http://localhost:3000
```

Endpoints

GET /

Description

Returns a welcome message.

Common Language Capabilities

Some languages are specialized, such as COBOL and SQL. For example, COBOL is used for developing applications for data processing. As for SQL, it is about writing scripts to manage databases.

Yet most languages are general purpose, which means you can write many types of applications. These may be a video game, business application, or an analytics tool.

A general-purpose language will also have some common capabilities:

- Loops, conditionals, and variables
- Data structures
- Functions

Let's take a look at how GitHub Copilot can help with these.

Loops, Conditionals, and Variables

The following help with the logic and data flows of a program:

- *Loops:* These iterate blocks of code. They can be for a specific number of times (a `for` loop) or when a condition is met (a `while` loop).

- *Conditionals:* These make decisions in a program, such as with an if/then structure.
- *Variables:* These represent values in a program.

You will find these in any language, including specialized versions. These programming structures are fundamental for software development.

GitHub Copilot usually creates loops, conditionals, and variables for you using the underlying LLM. Exercise 6.3 shows the process for this.

EXERCISE 6.3

Creating a Program with Loops, Conditionals, and Variables

1. Click the Copilot icon on the top-right side of the screen in VS Code.

2. Select Open Chat.

3. Use this prompt: *Write a program in Python that guesses a randomly generated number between 1 and 10.*

4. The following image shows the response from GitHub Copilot. It imports the random package to create random numbers. Next, there is a function that includes two variables. One is for the number to guess, and the other is for the user's guess. After this, there is a while loop to see if there is a match. This structure is the best choice since there is no fixed number for the iterations.

```python
import random

def guess_number():
    number_to_guess = random.randint(1, 10)
    guess = None

    print("I have generated a number between 1 and 10. Ca

    while guess != number_to_guess:
        guess = int(input("Enter your guess: "))

        if guess < number_to_guess:
            print("Too low! Try again.")
        elif guess > number_to_guess:
            print("Too high! Try again.")
        else:
```

Data Structures

A *data structure* is a format for organizing, storing, and processing data. This is an attribute of all languages.

A common data structure is an *array*. This contains a list of data, which is identified by an index. An example is {10, 20, 30, 40, 50}. For this, the index is from 0 to 4, and you will associate it with a variable. This could be something like array_list[]. Then, if you want to reference a data item—say for 2—you can use array_list[2], which has a value of 30.

With GitHub Copilot, you can create an array with a prompt like this:

Create an array of integers from 1 to 10.

Another type of data structure is a *hash table*. It stores key-value pairs for looking up, inserting, and deleting data. For this, there will be a hash function to calculate the index or code from a key. This is where the value will be stored.

Here's an example of a prompt:

Write a C++ program using unordered_map *to manage a simple order system for a bookstore.*

GitHub Copilot will write the code and use unordered_map, which is the C++ standard library for hash tables.

Functions

A *function* is a block of code that performs a task. By using functions, you can break down your code into manageable parts. This can help with organization, readability, and maintainability. Functions can also be reusable.

Unfortunately, they can also be written poorly. Ironically, functions can sometimes lead to disorganization and poor code quality.

Before using GitHub Copilot to create functions, it's a good idea to understand the best practices:

- **Single responsibility principle:** Each function should perform a single task.
- **Naming:** The name of a function should be clear and descriptive.
- **Concise:** A function should not be long. Otherwise, it can be too complex and tougher to maintain.
- **Values:** Use parameters for inputs and return values for outputs. This allows for predictability.

In light of this, here are some sample prompts:

Create a function named calculate_average *that computes the average of a list of numbers.*

Generate a function called `fetch_user_data` *that retrieves user information from a database using a user ID as a parameter.*

Write a function called `convert_to_celsius` *that accepts a temperature in Fahrenheit and returns the equivalent in Celsius.*

Code Translation

Code translation is about converting the codebase from one programming language to another. This is also referred to as *transpilation*. This process is common for modernization of legacy systems.

But code translation can be challenging, as each programming language has its own syntax and structures. For example, there are fundamental differences between object-oriented and functional languages. Each language will also have their own libraries, packages, and APIs. There will also be differences with memory management and optimization approaches.

In other words, code translation is often much more than converting the commands. There is the need for customization. Regardless, GitHub Copilot can still be helpful with code translation—at least for the initial steps. For example, you could start with a prompt like this:

Translate this Java code to C#, following C# conventions and best practices for exception handling.

True, the code translation will likely be far from perfect. But it still should help to save time with the process, in terms of making the initial conversions. You can then use GitHub Copilot for refining the translation, such as with refactoring (covered in the next section of this chapter) and testing (covered in the next chapter).

Code Refactoring

Code refactoring describes the process of optimizing existing code. This is done without changing the underlying functionality. With code refactoring, you are improving the readability and maintainability of the code, as well as lowering its complexity.

A key part of code refactoring is to root out the *code smells*, which is poorly designed code. They do not break the execution of a program, but they often can lead to problems like poor performance or technical debt.

Another important benefit of code refactoring is that it helps to enhance system design. This allows for accelerated development of new features and fewer bugs. Regardless, the code refactoring process can be challenging for developers. In the next few sections, you see how GitHub Copilot can help with the process.

Extract Method

Sometimes a function or method will be too long or have multiple tasks. This can make the code too complicated and not reusable.

Here's an example:

```
def calculate_price(items):
    total_amount = 0
    for item in items:
        price = item['price'] * item['quantity']
        if item['quantity'] > 10:
            price *= 0.9  # This is a discount for volume purchases
        total += price
    return total
```

This function actually has two main tasks: computing the individual item price and summing the total. To refactor this, you can use the *extract method*, which will rearrange the function or method into one or more functions or methods.

This is the updated code:

```
def calculate_item_price(item):
    price = item["price"] * item["quantity"]
    return price * 0.9 if item["quantity"] > 10 else price # This is the
discount for volume purchases
def calculate_total_price(items):
    return sum(calculate_item_price(item) for item in items)
```

With Copilot, you can create prompts for the extract method:

> *Analyze this function and suggest code blocks that can be extracted into separate methods to improve readability.*

> *Refactor this method to ensure it follows the Single Responsibility Principle by extracting code snippets into new methods.*

Decomposing Conditionals

Suppose you are writing an application that has access control. It's for permissions based on the role, subscription tier, two-factor authentication status, account age, and region.

Here's some code for it:

```
def access_control(role, subscription, two_factor, age, region):
    if role == "admin" or (role == "moderator" and two_factor):
        return "Full access granted"

    if role == "user":
        if subscription == "enterprise" and (two_factor or age > 1):
            return "Enterprise access"
        if subscription == "premium":
            return "Premium access" if two_factor else "Enable 2FA"
        if subscription == "free":
            return "Basic access" if age > 1 and region == "US" else
              "Limited access"
    return "Access denied"
```

This code works fine, but it is far from well written. Because of the nested conditionals, it can be difficult to follow the logic of the code. It would likely require time-consuming analysis of the flows to get a sense of how this works. It could also be difficult to test.

A better approach is to rewrite this code by using a technique called *decomposing conditionals*. This breaks the code down into smaller functions that are focused on specific conditions.

Exercise 6.4 shows how to do this using GitHub Copilot.

EXERCISE 6.4

Decomposing Conditionals

1. Click the Copilot icon on the top-right side of the screen in VS Code.

2. Select Open Chat.

3. Highlight the code.

4. Use this prompt: *Decompose the conditionals for this code. Extract logic for determining admin or moderator access, enterprise access, premium access, and free access into well-named functions. Ensure the main function remains concise and only calls these helper functions. Maintain existing functionality while improving readability and modularity.*

5. The following image shows the response from GitHub Copilot. It shows a list of concise functions that carry out the logic for the application.

```
def has_enterprise_access(subscription, two_factor, age):
    return subscription == "enterprise" and (two_factor o

def has_premium_access(subscription, two_factor):
    return subscription == "premium" and two_factor

def has_free_access(subscription, age, region):
    return subscription == "free" and age > 1 and region

def access_control(role, subscription, two_factor, age, r
    if is_admin_or_moderator(role, two_factor):
        return "Full access granted"

    if role == "user":
        if has_enterprise_access(subscription, two_fact
            return "Enterprise access"
```

Deciphering Ninja Code

Ninja code refers to programming that is highly cryptic and complex. It can be almost impossible to understand.

This is an example:

```
_ = lambda s: ''.join(chr((ord(c.lower()) - 97 + 13) % 26 + 97) if c.isalpha()
else "*" if c.isspace() else c for c in s)
```

Any idea what this means? It would likely take quite a while to figure this out—even though it's only one line of code.

But with GitHub Copilot, you can decipher this by using the /explain command in Chat. This is the response:

> *This code snippet is a concise way to apply the ROT13 cipher to alphabetic characters, replace whitespace with asterisks, and leave other characters unchanged.*

Identifying Dead Code

As codebases grow, there is often *dead code*. This includes functions, variables, or code blocks that no longer function in an application. It's often due to the changing requirements.

Even though dead code does not impact the functionality of the program, it can mean bloat and complexity of the codebase. This can make it challenging for maintainability and upgrades.

When using GitHub Copilot, these are some prompts to detect dead code:

Identify unused functions in this codebase.

Highlight variables that are declared but never used.

Suggest refactoring opportunities to remove dead code.

However, you need to be careful with these. With a fixed context window for the LLM, GitHub Copilot may not understand the entire codebase. Even with a smaller codebase, there can still be challenges, such as with hallucinations.

Data Creation

Creating data is useful for testing applications. Some of the use cases include evaluating edge cases, authentication, performance evaluation, data visualization, usability, integration, and migration. But this type of data can also be used for building AI models.

Another key benefit of creating data is privacy. The information will not contain any sensitive details. But there is a major drawback with creating data—that is, it can be time-consuming to generate. Yet GitHub Copilot can assist with the process.

To see how, consider an example. Suppose you are creating an application and you want to test it with sample user IDs and passwords. This is the prompt:

Create demo data that is realistic for two IDs and passwords.

This is the response from Copilot:

```
[
    {
        "id": 1,
        "username": "johndoe",
        "password": "Jd0e!2025"
    },
    {
        "id": 2,
        "username": "janedoe",
        "password": "JaNe#2025"
    }
]
```

It not only creates useful data but also does this in JSON format. This will make it easier to use in your application. General-purpose LLMs like ChatGPT and Claude can be useful when creating data as well. You can have something like this:

Create demo data for five IDs and passwords. Convert this into a CSV file.

However, with GitHub Copilot, you cannot create a file.

Database Schemas and SQL

A *database schema* defines how data is organized in a database. It has information about the tables, fields, data types, and relationships. Think of a database schema as a template for creating and managing a database. If it is well designed, it results in efficient data organization and minimal redundancy.

But the process for creating a database schema can be tricky. You need to understand database administration, as well as the particular domain.

With GitHub Copilot, you can generate effective database schemas. These are some prompts:

Create a database schema for a normalized relational database. It is for a social media site that has tables for users, posts, comments, likes, and followers.

This is what it suggests for the users table:

```
CREATE TABLE Users (
    user_id INT PRIMARY KEY AUTO_INCREMENT,
    username VARCHAR(50) NOT NULL UNIQUE,
    email VARCHAR(100) NOT NULL UNIQUE,
    password_hash VARCHAR(255) NOT NULL,
    created_at TIMESTAMP DEFAULT CURRENT_TIMESTAMP
);
```

You can also use GitHub Copilot for *structured query language (SQL)*. This is a scripting language for managing relational databases, such to create, modify, and query data.

GitHub Copilot is fairly good with SQL. A key reason is that there is a huge amount of this code in public repositories.

Here is a sample prompt:

Write a SQL query to retrieve customer names and their order details. Use INNER JOIN on the customers and orders table. The customers table has columns for customer_id, name, and email. The orders table has columns for order_id, customer_id, order_date, and total_amount.

This is the response from GitHub Copilot:

```
SELECT
    customers.name AS customer_name,
    orders.order_id,
    orders.order_date,
    orders.total_amount
FROM
    customers
INNER JOIN
    orders
ON
    customers.customer_id = orders.customer_id;
```

Data Conversion

Data conversion is about transforming data from one format to another. This requires understanding the compatibility intricacies between the two systems.

For GitHub Copilot, this is a straightforward process. Suppose you have a CSV file with customer profiles. This is an example:

```
101,Alice,Smith,alice.smith@example.com,555-1234,"123 Maple St, Springfield",Springfield,IL,62701
```

Exercise 6.5 shows how to do the conversion in GitHub Copilot.

EXERCISE 6.5

Data Conversion

1. Click the Copilot icon on the top-right side of the screen in VS Code.

2. Select Open Chat.

3. Load the CSV file into your workspace.

4. Select it to make it the current file.

5. Use this prompt: *Convert this to XML.*

6. The following image shows the response from GitHub Copilot.

Here is the XML representation of the provided CSV data:

```xml
<Customers>
    <Customer>
        <CustomerID>101</CustomerID>
        <FirstName>Alice</FirstName>
        <LastName>Smith</LastName>
        <Email>alice.smith@example.com</Email>
        <PhoneNumber>555-1234</PhoneNumber>
        <Address>123 Maple St, Springfield</Address>
        <City>Springfield</City>
        <State>IL</State>
        <ZIPCode>62701</ZIPCode>
    </Customer>
```

Debugging

Various research studies show that developers spend about 35 to 50 percent of their time debugging software.[i] But depending on the complexity of the project, the rate could be as much as 75 percent.[ii] This comes to about 1,500 hours per year.

Debugging is one area in which GitHub can greatly increase developer productivity. It can help with virtually any type of bug. However, there are some instances in which the compiler will likely be a better option:

- *Syntax errors:* These describe issues with the grammar of the language, such as unmatched parentheses or incorrect indention.

- *Runtime errors:* These happen during the code execution. Examples include bad null pointer references or division by zero. You can use a compiler's inspect tools to address this type of error.

- *Concurrency errors:* These occur during the concurrent execution of a program, such as with deadlocks. A dynamic analysis tool in an IDE can monitor the threads to detect this type of error.

- *Memory errors:* These describe problems with memory allocation and deallocation, such as memory leaks or buffer overflows. You need a specialized debugger for these.

Then what are the types of errors best suited for GitHub Copilot? I already mentioned some of them, like code smells and optimizing performance with refactoring.

But GitHub Copilot can also be useful with *logic errors*. This is a problem with the structure of the code that generates an incorrect result or unintended output—without crashing the application.

Consider this example:

```
def is_even(number):
    return number % 2 == 1

# Test the function
print(is_even(4))
print(is_even(7))
```

The is_even function checks if a number is even. However, this will get the wrong result because of a logic error.

Exercise 6.6 shows how to fix this using GitHub Copilot.

EXERCISE 6.6

Fixing Logic Errors

1. Click the Copilot icon on the top-right side of the screen in VS Code.

2. Select Open Chat.

3. Highlight the code snippet.

4. Use this prompt: */fix + /explain*.

5. The following image shows the response from GitHub Copilot. It identifies that there is a logic error and provides the corrected code.

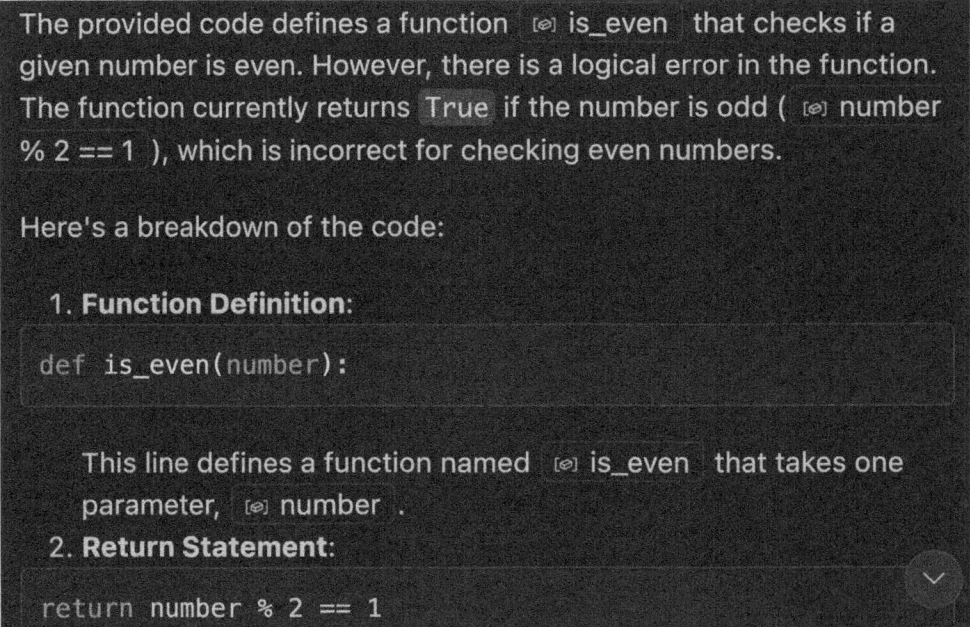

6. Besides using Chat, you can use inline chat. You activate this with Command+I on the Mac or Ctrl+I in Windows. With this, you will get an explanation, but not the updated code. You need to use Chat for this.

7. You can also highlight the code snippet and click the right mouse button. Select Copilot from the menu and then click Fix.

You can also use GitHub Copilot for *exception handling*. This is where your code will manage errors or unexpected outcomes. This means the program will continue to run despite the problems. Depending on the language, exception handling will have commands like `try`, `catch`, and `finally`, which apply to certain blocks of the code.

Here is a sample prompt for this:

Add exception error handling to this function.

Finally, another way GitHub Copilot can assist with debugging is when you get a long error message, which may go on for several pages. This can be very difficult to figure out. It often takes lots of research, such as on Google and Stack Overflow. But Copilot can be particularly helpful since it can detect the complex patterns. In fact, when you get this kind of error, you can cut and paste it into Chat. Copilot will understand that it's an error message and provide a response.

Regular Expressions (Regex)

A *regulator expression (regex)* is a sequence of characters that represents a pattern. They are used for scenarios like validating email formats, searching for specific phrases, or extracting information.

Take this regex: `'^\d{3}-\d{2}-\d{4}$'`. This pattern matches strings formatted as a Social Security number (SSN) in the United States. The `^` character specifies the position at the start of the string. Then the `\d{X}` format is for a fixed number of digits, which are separated with the `-` character. Finally, the `$` character identifies the position at the end of the string.

Here are some sample prompts for regex statements:

Generate a regex that matches a five-digit ZIP code.

Develop a regex to extract URLs from any given text.

Construct a regex to match dates in the format "MM/DD/YYYY."

GitHub Copilot can also decipher regex patterns. Here's a sample prompt:

Explain the following regex pattern: `^(?=.*[A-Z])(?=.*\d)[A-Za-z\d]{8,}$`

This validates a password that's at least eight characters long, contains at least one uppercase letter, and has at least one digit.

The Software Development Life Cycle (SDLC)

The *software development life cycle (SDLC)* describes the main phases in developing applications. They include the following:

- Requirements analysis
- Design and development
- Testing and quality assurance
- Deployment
- Maintenance and support

Figure 6.1 shows the process in a chart.

With a well-defined SDLC process, there are some key benefits. First, the quality of the application should be improved. Next, a clear roadmap will help with project planning, as well as allow for better use of resources and time management. Finally, there should be enhanced communication. The team will know what to do and when to do it, which will help to keep the project on track.

Yet the SDLC process is not without its challenges. In some cases, there can be too much planning. This can lead to the proverbial "analysis paralysis." The team may get frustrated with the lack of progress and so will the client or stakeholders.

A leader knows when to make a decision and move on the project. Besides, it's important to allow for flexibility with the plan. It's impossible to know everything upfront with a

FIGURE 6.1   The software development life cycle (SDLC)

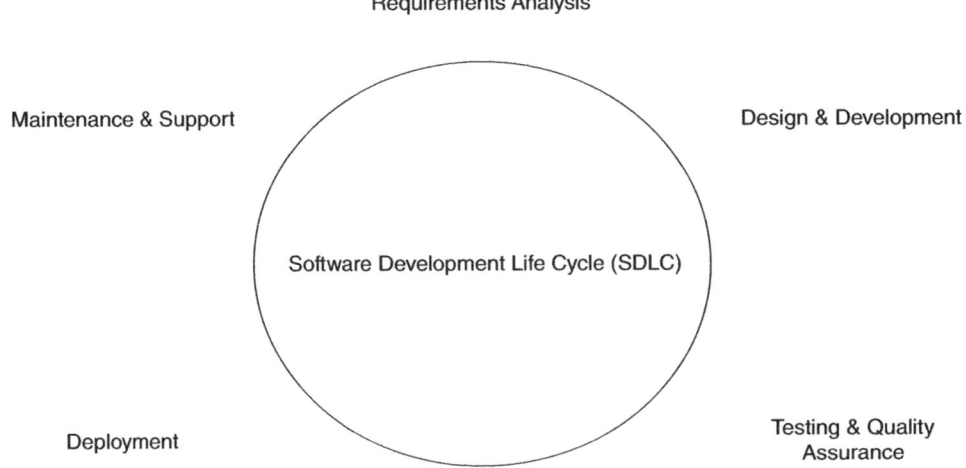

complex project. The flexibility will also allow for more innovation and creativity. For the most part, an effective SDLC process is a balancing act.

There are different approaches too:

- *Waterfall model*: This is a traditional model, used during the early days of computers. It tends to have detailed instructions, and each phase must be completed before going to the next one. The waterfall method is usually for when a project needs to be well-defined and the requirements are not expected to have many changes. However, this structured approach can mean much less flexibility. It can also lead to delays and higher costs.

- *Agile model*: This approach emerged in 2001, in which 17 software developers published a document called the "Agile Manifesto." It included four core values and 12 principles, with a focus on fast, flexible, and incremental development. The approach involves a team that will deliver software in *sprints*, which are followed up with user feedback. The agile method is usually for projects where speed is essential and the initial requirements are difficult to determine.

- *Big bang model*: This approach is more unstructured. It's when a software developer will jump into a project with little planning. This is usually for small projects that are not complex.

- *DevOps*: This combines software development and operations teams, which helps to improve collaboration. DevOps usually involves frequent testing, automated deployments—such as with continuous integration/continuous delivery (CI/CD) pipelines—and strong monitoring. This approach is usually best for projects that require ongoing updates, which are common for cloud applications. It's also typical to combine DevOps with agile methods.

- *Lean development*: This is about producing software that attempts to maximize value and minimize waste. This approach is based on methods for improving manufacturing. Some of the key principles for lean development involve the delivery of value early, continuous improvement, having fast feedback loops, and promoting collaboration across teams.

With GitHub Copilot, you can get recommendations on the best SDLC approach for a project. This is a sample prompt:

Below is a description of an app we are creating [paste the description]. Recommend the best SDLC model, such as waterfall, agile, big bang, DevOps, or lean. Explain your reasoning for your choice.

In the next few sections, you'll look at how GitHub Copilot can assist with the different phases of the SDLC process. I do not cover the design and development stage, since I already covered much of this in the chapter so far. The same goes for maintenance and support. This is mostly about correcting bugs after an application has been deployed.

Testing and quality assurance are covered in the next chapter.

Requirements Analysis

Requirements analysis is about collecting, documenting, and managing the needs of stakeholders about a software project.

Unfortunately, this can be extremely challenging. There are plenty of examples where poor requirements analysis has led to failed projects. Some have been unmitigated disasters, like the following:

- **FBI's virtual case file project:** Launched in 2000, this initiative was focused on modernizing the organization's case management system. However, the requirements were exceedingly complex and confusing. There were also many changes. By 2005, the FBI abandoned the project after spending $170 million.[iii]

- **California DMV's IT modernization project:** The organization started this in 2006.[iv] But the requirements proved to be overly cumbersome. It did not help that the existing system was complex. After millions were spent on the project, the DMV abandoned it in 2013.

There are several types of software requirements. Here are the main ones:

- *Functional requirements*: These define specific functions or capabilities of a system, say the underlying calculations, data processing, and user experience.

- *Non-functional requirements*: These identify the criteria to judge the operation of a system. This is usually about performance, reliability, and security.

- *Domain requirements*: These are about a particular category, such as finance, legal, marketing and so on.

With GitHub Copilot, you can generate these types of requirements. Exercise 6.7 shows the steps for this.

EXERCISE 6.7

Creating Requirements

1. Click the Copilot icon on the top-right side of the screen in VS Code.

2. Select Open Chat.

3. Select a file that has notes for the requirements of your application. This can be a text or markdown file.

4. Select a more advanced model, such as Claude 3.7 Sonnet, Gemini 2.0 Flash, or o1. These should do better in processing and writing the requirements.

5. Use this prompt: *Write functional requirements for this file.*

6. The following image shows the response from GitHub Copilot.

Functional Requirements

1. **User Authentication**
   ◦ Users must log in using their company credentials.
   ◦ Authentication should be performed through the company's LDAP system.
   ◦ Successful authentication should redirect users to the main dashboard.
   ◦ Login process should be completed in under 2 seconds.
2. **Dashboard Access**
   ◦ Authenticated users should have access to the main dashboard.
   ◦ The dashboard should display relevant user-specific information.

What specific features should be included?

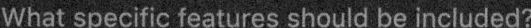

Deployment

It's common for applications to be deployed to a cloud platform, such as AWS, Azure, or Google Cloud. They provide scale, security, and high availability. These cloud platforms also come with many tools and services for application deployment.

Deployment can be done all at once or rolled out gradually. It depends on factors like the need for testing and mitigating downtime, such as for mission-critical applications.

To automate and orchestrate the deployment, there are various tools and approaches. *Continuous integration/continuous deployment (CI/CD)* allows for creating automation scripts for faster and more reliable software releases, such as for the build, test, and deployment process. Then there is *Kubernetes*, which packages applications into containers. Often, this is done using Docker. The containers contain their own IT environment, which allows for easier updates and scaling.

The GitHub Copilot for Azure extension can help with deploying applications to the Azure platform, which is covered in Chapter 2.

Here are sample prompts:

@azure What types of application hosting options does Azure provide?

@azure Create a script to deploy a web app that will run in Python.

@azure Could you help me create and deploy a simple Flask website by using an azd template?

GitHub Copilot can also help with non-Azure deployment. Here are some prompts:

Create a Dockerfile for a Node.js app for AWS. I want the script to have this deployed using a load balancer.

What are the steps to create a CI/CD pipeline using AWS?

Make a GitHub Actions workflow to deploy a Python function using Google Cloud Functions.

REST API

In Chapter 3, you saw how the GitHub Copilot REST API—or productivity API—can help an organization evaluate the impact of this tool. It will show various metrics, such as for the number of suggestions generated and the acceptance rates.

To create a program using the REST API, you can use any language that makes HTTP requests. But GitHub has client libraries—called Octokit—to help streamline the process. They are for JavaScript/TypeScript, Ruby, and .NET. There are also third-party libraries available, such as for Go, Java, and Python.

You can get access to the endpoints for the categories of enterprises, organizations, and teams for GitHub Copilot. Here are the formats:

```
GET /enterprises/{enterprise}/copilot/metrics
GET /orgs/{org}/copilot/metrics
GET /orgs/{org}/teams/{team_slug}/copilot/metrics
```

Where you see { }, you will fill in the name of your enterprise, organization, or team. This is an example—using curl—for an organization called XYZCorp.

```
curl -L \
  -H "Accept: application/vnd.github+json" \
  -H "Authorization: Bearer YOUR_TOKEN" \
  https://api.github.com/orgs/XYZCorp/copilot/metrics
```

There are various open-source projects that generate reports using the GitHub Copilot REST API. One is GitHub Copilot Metrics Viewer, which creates charts for different metrics. You can find the project at `https://github.com/github-copilot-resources/copilot-metrics-viewer?tab=readme-ov-file`.

Summary

In this chapter, you learned about the many ways you can use GitHub Copilot. Just some include learning languages, creating documentation, using code refactoring, generating data, and debugging.

You also looked at how you can use GitHub Copilot to improve the SDLC process. The chapter ended with a review of the REST API.

In the next chapter, you learn about software testing.

Exam Essentials

Understand how to debug and refactor code using GitHub Copilot.   You can use this tool to identify logic errors, detect dead code, and refactor complex code blocks. This will help to improve code quality, readability, and maintainability.

Understand that you can use GitHub Copilot as a learning tool.   You can use prompts to ask questions about a language or framework. This can also be personalized, such as by having GitHub Copilot show examples of code snippets. It also can create study guides and code challenges.

Understand how you can use GitHub Copilot for documentation.   It can evaluate the context of your code and generate documentation, such as a user guide. You can also generate comments.

Learn about the data creation capabilities of GitHub Copilot.   You can create realistic test data for your application, such as for logins. You can do this in various formats like JSON. You can also use GitHub Copilot to create database schemas, such as for SQL scripts.

Know about the SDLC process with GitHub Copilot.   You should understand the main steps: requirements analysis, design and development, testing and quality assurance, deployment, and maintenance and support. You should also know how you can use GitHub Copilot for this process, such as using prompts to help deploy an application.

Understand the REST API.   You should know that this can provide access to metrics about the usage of GitHub Copilot. You should also understand that you can access the endpoints for enterprises, organizations, and teams.

Review Questions

1. In what ways can you use GitHub Copilot to learn a new programming language?

    A. It can write long-form content.

    B. It can only do this using the default model in the system.

    C. It can create personalized examples and explanations.

    D. It can search the Internet for tutorials.

2. Among these options, which is not a common developer use case for GitHub Copilot?

    A. Getting help with deployment to Azure

    B. Creating files that have generated code

    C. Creating data

    D. Debugging

3. What is a benefit of using GitHub Copilot to create documentation?

    A. You cannot use the tool for this.

    B. It will use the whole codebase as context.

    C. It will add images.

    D. It can generate documentation for an API that's in a Markdown format.

4. What type of errors is GitHub Copilot best suited to handle?

    A. Logic errors

    B. Syntax errors

    C. Memory errors

    D. Runtime errors

5. What kind of data can GitHub Copilot create?

    A. Randomized data

    B. Synthetic data that can be used for testing

    C. Sensor data

    D. Real-time data for streaming

6. In which phase of the SDLC process can you use GitHub Copilot?

    A. Requirements analysis

    B. Design and development

    C. Deployment

    D. All of the phases

7. What can you do with the REST API or productivity API for GitHub Copilot?

  A. Get metrics on the usage of GitHub Copilot

  B. Create AI applications

  C. Access different AI models

  D. Integrate with third-party applications

8. What can you do with code translation in GitHub Copilot?

  A. You can convert text into another spoken language.

  B. You can create an API.

  C. You can convert code from one language into another one.

  D. You can integrate with third-party applications.

9. Among the following SDLC models, which one is best for software projects where there are frequent updates and collaboration between development and operations teams?

  A. DevOps

  B. Agile

  C. Lean development

  D. Waterfall

10. For GitHub Copilot, which capability is about optimizing code without changing its functionality?

  A. Automated deployment

  B. Code refactoring

  C. Waterfall

  D. Continuous development

11. When using GitHub Copilot, what is a drawback when using code refactoring?

  A. The inability to format the code

  B. No option to use another AI model

  C. The conflict with the proxy filter

  D. Limited understanding of the entire codebase

12. How can GitHub Copilot help with creating database schemas?

  A. You can use the SQL extension.

  B. The training data does not include SQL content.

  C. It can create scripts to define tables, fields, and relationships.

  D. It is restricted because of security reasons.

13. How can GitHub Copilot help with writing requirements for a software project?

   A. This is beyond the scope of the tool.

   B. It can only write non-functional requirements.

   C. It can be automatically generated by adding notes to your prompt.

   D. It is integrated with Microsoft Word.

14. For these options, which best describes the extract method that GitHub Copilot can help with?

   A. Combining multiple methods into one

   B. Moving functions into separate files

   C. Dividing a large function into smaller ones for better clarity

   D. Removing all comments to reduce clutter

15. What is the endpoint when using the REST API for an enterprise?

   A. `GET /enterprises/{enterprise}/copilot/metrics`.

   B. `GET /copilot/usage/enterprise`.

   C. `GET /orgs/{org}/copilot/metrics`.

   D. `GET /enterprises`.

16. How can GitHub Copilot help with deploying applications onto the Azure cloud platform?

   A. You need to do this in Azure, not GitHub Copilot.

   B. You need to use the GitHub Copilot REST API.

   C. You can use the GitHub Copilot for Azure extension.

   D. You need to use GitHub Kubernetes.

17. How can GitHub Copilot interpret ninja code?

   A. By using code conversion

   B. By using pseudocode

   C. By using debugging techniques

   D. By using `/explain`

18. What command do you use in GitHub Copilot to understand regular expressions?

   A. `/regex`

   B. `/regexplain`

   C. `/explain`

   D. `/debug`

19. What is a disadvantage in using GitHub Copilot to detect dead code?

   A. It may not have the full context of the codebase.

   B. Dead code is not caught in the proxy filter.

   C. You need to use a vector database.

   D. It can introduce security vulnerabilities.

20. Which of the following can you use to fix a logic error in your code?

   A. `/logicfix`

   B. `/test + /evaluate`

   C. `/fix + /logic`

   D. `/fix + /explain`

Notes

1. Amcqueue (March 2017). The Debugging Mindset. https://queue.acm.org/detail.cfm?id=3068 754 (Accessed 3 March 2025).

2. Coralogix Blog (February 2015). This Is What Your Developers Are Doing 75% of the Time, and This Is the Cost You Pay. https://coralogix.com/blog/this-is-what-your-developers-are-doing-75-of-the-time-and-this-is-the-cost-you-pay/ (Accessed 27 February 2025).

3. InfoWorld.com (March 2005). Anatomy of an IT Disaster: How the FBI Blew It. https://www.infoworld.com/article/2214992/anatomy-of-an-it-disaster-how-the-fbi-blew-it.html (Accessed 4 March 2025).

4. IEEE Spectrum (February 2013). Déjà Vu All Over Again: California's DMV IT Project Cancelled. https://spectrum.ieee.org/dj-vu-all-over-again-californias-dmv-it-project-cancelled (Accessed 4 March 2025).

Chapter

7

Testing and Privacy Considerations

THE GITHUB COPILOT EXAM OBJECTIVES COVERED IN THIS CHAPTER INCLUDE, BUT ARE NOT LIMITED TO, THE FOLLOWING:

✔ **Domain 6: Testing with GitHub Copilot**

- Describe the options for generating testing for your code
    - Describe how GitHub Copilot can be used to add unit tests, integration tests, and other test types to your code
    - Explain how GitHub Copilot can assist in identifying edge cases and suggesting tests to address them
- Enhance code quality through testing
    - Describe how to improve the effectiveness of existing tests with GitHub Copilot's suggestions
    - Describe how to generate boilerplate code for various tests types using GitHub Copilot
    - Explain how GitHub Copilot can help write assertions for different testing scenarios
- Leverage GitHub Copilot for security and performance
    - Describe how GitHub Copilot can learn from existing tests to suggest improvements and identify potential issues in the code
    - Explain how to use GitHub Copilot Enterprise for collaborative code reviews, leveraging security best practices, and performance considerations
    - Explain how GitHub Copilot can identify potential security vulnerabilities in your code
    - Describe how GitHub Copilot can suggest code optimizations for improved performance

✔ **Domain 7: Privacy fundamentals and context exclusions**

- Describe the different SKUs for GitHub Copilot

  - Describe the different SKUs and the privacy considerations for GitHub Copilot

  - Describe the different code suggestion configuration options on the organization level

  - Describe the GitHub Copilot Editor config file

- Identify content exclusions

  - Describe how to configure content exclusions in a repository and organization

  - Explain the effects of content exclusions

  - Explain the limitations of content exclusions

  - Describe the ownership of GitHub Copilot outputs

- Safeguards

  - Describe the duplication detector filter

  - Explain contractual protection

  - Explain how to configure GitHub Copilot settings on GitHub.com

  - Enabling/disabling duplication detection

  - Enabling/disabling prompt and suggestion collection

  - Describe security checks and warnings

- Troubleshooting

  - Explain how to solve the issue if code suggestions are not showing in your editor for some files

  - Explain why context exclusions may not be applied

  - Explain how to trigger GitHub Copilot when suggestions are either absent or not ideal

  - Explain steps for context exclusions in code editors

This chapter covers the last two domains for the exam. One is for testing using GitHub Copilot. The chapter begins by explaining the topic, with a brief history as well as different approaches, such as unit testing and integration. I show how to use GitHub Copilot to write these types of tests as well as the best practices. You also look at how to use the /tests slash command and how to create custom prompts.

The next domain covered in this chapter is about privacy and content exclusions. The chapter starts by discussing the commitment and vision of GitHub's approach to privacy. You then look at the various features, such as setting privacy configurations, exporting data, excluding files, using audit logs, and working with policy management.

Background on Testing

Software testing is about verifying if an application does what it is intended to do. This is a major part of the SDLC process, including *quality assurance (QA)*. This ensures that the software meets requirements and quality standards.

How is this different from software testing? Testing is primarily focused on debugging the software and evaluating the impact of different scenarios, which comes after the design and development phase of the SDLC process. QA is also done in this stage. But it is also something that is involved with the phases for requirements analysis, deployment, and maintenance and support. The goal is to eliminate defects, such as by improving processes, approaches, and methodologies.

As should be no surprise, testing has been around since the emergence of software. In the late 1940s, computer scientist Tom Kilburn essentially invented the field when he wrote the first software program, which was to perform mathematical calculations.[1] He debugged the code to make sure it was generating the correct responses.

Until the 1970s, debugging was the main approach to testing. But as programs got larger and more complicated, there needed to be better methods. The result was the development of modern testing techniques. The focus was on evaluating how an application would work in a real-world environment. This also involved QA to make sure that the software met the needs of customers.

Another trend was the use of automated testing tools. Earlier versions would record and playback keystrokes and processes, such as to evaluate a graphical user interface (GUI).

By the 1990s, there was another method of test automation—the use of scripting tools. These allowed for much more intricate testing. One of the most popular tools was Selenium, which helped with web-based applications. A key to its success was that it allowed for using Java, Python, and Ruby to create the scripts.

There would then be another important evolution with test automation tools, which included comprehensive frameworks and libraries. They could manage highly sophisticated automation scripts.

As for the latest trend in automation, it is with AI tools. AI is dramatically impacting this category. Besides GitHub Copilot, most other AI coding tools have testing capabilities.

Approaches to Testing

At a high level, there are two main approaches to testing. It can be either done manually or by using automated tools. Of course, both are critical for the success of testing. With manual testing, there is the benefit of human intuition, creativity, experience, and expert judgment. As for automated tools, they are quick and can evaluate many edge cases. They are also effective with tedious tasks.

But there are many other aspects to testing. For example, there are a myriad of methodologies available, such as unit testing and integration testing.

Unit Testing

Unit testing involves testing a small functional unit of the codebase. You initially write the test in code and then run it every time there is a change. This allows for quickly catching issues or bugs. You also typically write multiple tests for each of the functions, so as to cover the various scenarios and edge cases.

Besides early detection of problems with the code, there are other benefits of unit testing:

- **Code quality:** It should improve significantly. The focus is on making sure that the application meets the requirements.
- **Improved documentation:** The reason for this is that you evaluate different examples of how the software is supposed to be used.
- **Refactoring:** Unit tests help identify areas in which to optimize the code.
- **Integration:** Once you understand how each of the units work, it is easier to understand the relationships between them. This can further help improve the quality of the code.

Unit testing also supports *test-driven development (TDD)*. This is where you begin testing before writing the code.

Suppose you are writing a function for calculating the sales tax for an ecommerce application. You will first write a unit test to evaluate the accurate results. You will then write the minimal code for the function to pass the tests. Once all the conditions have been met, you may want to further refactor the code. With TDD, you generally are writing more reliable and maintainable applications.

Yet this does not imply that you should write unit tests or use TDD for every block of code. After all, these techniques take time and planning. Sometimes a code block is fairly straightforward and needs only a quick manual review. In other cases, the review is about the look and feel of the UI, not the underlying logic of the application. In fact, when it comes to working with complex legacy systems, unit tests may not be effective.

There are other drawbacks to using unit testing:

- **Crafting the tests:** This can be far from easy. You need to write clear unit tests that focus on the requirements of the software. But you also need to think about the edge cases. This process can be much more challenging when working with large projects.

- **Maintenance:** It can be time-consuming to update the unit tests.

- **Scope:** As unit testing is about focusing on small parts of the code, this can mean missing out on broader aspects of an application. To help with this, you can use integration tests, which are covered later in this chapter.

- **Bias:** Since developers often write the unit tests, this can mean that they have blind spots. In other words, they may be too close to the code.

Despite all these issues, unit tests are generally a good approach. But you need to be aware of some potential issues.

The next few sections take a look at other aspects of unit testing, including an example of how it works and a review of the best practices.

Example of a Unit Test

To better understand how unit testing works, consider the following example. Suppose you have a block of Python code that takes in a list of products and applies a tax calculation:

```python
def calculate_total_price(items, tax_rate):

    if not items:
        return 0.0

    subtotal = 0.0
    for item in items:
        subtotal += item["price"] * item["quantity"]

    total = subtotal * (1 + tax_rate)
    return round(total, 2)
```

For the unit testing, you will first determine what framework to use. This will have functions for creating test cases and helping with the evaluations.

Python has a variety of frameworks:

- `unittest`: This is a standard system built into the Python language.
- `doctest`: This uses docstrings to embed test examples.
- `Behave`: This is known as a behavior-driven development (BDD) framework, which allows for writing tests in natural language.

This example uses `unittest`.

Next, you write the test cases. These are the potential scenarios for your function. They will include common use cases, edge cases, and error conditions. For example, you can test for an empty list, zero quantity, zero price, and zero tax rate.

To implement the unit test, you write the following code:

```python
import unittest

class TestCalculateTotalPrice(unittest.TestCase):

    def test_empty_items(self):
        self.assertEqual(calculate_total_price([], 0.1), 0.0)

    def test_single_item(self):
        items = [{"price": 10.00, "quantity": 2}]
        self.assertEqual(calculate_total_price(items, 0.1), 22.0)

    def test_zero_quantity(self):
        items = [{"price": 10.00, "quantity": 0}]
        self.assertEqual(calculate_total_price(items, 0.1), 0.0)

    def test_zero_price(self):
        items = [{"price": 0.00, "quantity": 5}]
        self.assertEqual(calculate_total_price(items, 0.1), 0.0)

    def test_zero_tax_rate(self):
        items = [{"price": 10.00, "quantity": 2}]
        self.assertEqual(calculate_total_price(items, 0.0), 20.0)

if __name__ == '__main__':
    unittest.main()
```

There would likely be more test cases. But this code is meant to give you a general idea of how a unit test works.

For this code example, you first import `unittest`. Then you create a class that inherits the `unittest.TestCase` class, which has assertion methods. An *assertion method* verifies whether a condition is `true` or `false`.

The first one tests whether there are empty items. The `self.assertEqual` method checks to see if the output from `calculate_total_price`—in the original code block—matches the result, which is `0.0`. If it does, then there is an empty list.

There are assertion methods for the other test cases. You then run the tests to see if there are any that do not pass the conditions. You can then fix the problems and refactor the code.

Best Practices for Unit Testing

As noted, unit testing is not without its issues and difficulties. But there are some best practices to help out:

- **Paths:** As much as possible, try to anticipate the potential pathways for the code. This can take some time and planning, but it will mean having robust unit tests.

- **Assert once:** For each unit test, there should be only one outcome: true or false. If not, it will be difficult to interpret the results.

- **Independence:** One unit test should not rely on the outcome of another. This helps to avoid cascading failures. It will also allow for identifying the root cause of the problems.

- **Simplicity:** Unit tests should not involve complex logic. The focus is on being clear on what is being tested.

- **Test doubles:** If the code is using data for processing, you should use mocks, which are simulated actions. This means that the tests are focused on the behavior of the function, not outside factors.

Integration Testing

While unit testing focuses on parts of the codebase, *integration testing* is about evaluating all the components. It's focused on understanding the interactions, which are a common source of issues, bugs, and conflicts.

There are different methods for integration testing:

- **Big-bang integration testing:** You evaluate all the modules. However, this can make it difficult to isolate the causes of the issues.

- **Top-down integration testing:** You begin with the core modules and then work down from there. For these, you often do simulations by using mocks.

- **Bottom-up integration testing:** You can start with the more specialized modules and then work your way up. By using this method, you can spot core issues early in the process.

Automation tools for integration testing are usually more complex versus those for unit testing. There are open source platforms available, such as Selenium, SoapUI, MockServer, and Playwright. As for premium systems, examples include Parasoft SOAtest, LoadRunner, and Cantata++.

Next in this chapter, you learn how to use GitHub Copilot for unit testing and integration testing.

Testing Using GitHub Copilot

Testing when using GitHub Copilot is usually about unit tests. It can greatly speed up the process and provide a good start. It can create the boilerplate code, but it can also be customized according to a function or block of code.

However, GitHub Copilot may miss some edge cases. This is why it's important to review the code and see if there are other tests to add.

GitHub Copilot also provides different approaches for unit testing:

- Using /tests
- Using custom prompts

Using /tests

With the /tests slash command, GitHub Copilot will create unit tests for the selected code. This is the easiest approach. The slash command is available with Chat and inline chat.

Consider an example. The following is a simple function that performs a math operation with parameters for the operation and two variables:

```
def calculate(operation, a, b):
    if operation == 'add':
        return a + b
    elif operation == 'subtract':
        return a - b
    elif operation == 'multiply':
        return a * b
    elif operation == 'divide':
        if b == 0:
            raise ValueError("Cannot divide by zero")
        return a / b
    else:
        raise ValueError("Unsupported operation")
```

Exercise 7.1 shows the steps for using /tests with this function.

EXERCISE 7.1

Using the /tests Function

1. Save the function as a file in your IDE.

2. At the top of the screen, click the GitHub Copilot icon and select Open Chat.

3. Highlight the function with your mouse or select the name of the file, which is under the Ask Copilot input box.

4. Enter **/tests**.

5. The following image shows the unit tests.

```
 1+ import unittest
 2+ from test import calculate
 3+
 4+ class TestCalculate(unittest.TestCase):
 5+
 6+     def test_addition(self):
 7+         self.assertEqual(calculate('add', 2, 3), 5)
 8+         self.assertEqual(calculate('add', -1, 1), 0)
 9+         self.assertEqual(calculate('add', -1, -1), -2)
10+
11+     def test_subtraction(self):
12+         self.assertEqual(calculate('subtract', 3, 2),
13+         self.assertEqual(calculate('subtract', -1, 1),
14+         self.assertEqual(calculate('subtract', -1, -1)
15+
16+     def test_multiplication(self):
17+         self.assertEqual(calculate('multiply', 2, 3),
```

6. If you do not know how to run a unit test, you can ask GitHub the following: *How do I run this in my IDE?*

7. With the unit tests, you will create a file for them. This example calls it `test_calculate.py`.

8. Go to the terminal and enter this: `python -m unittest discover -s 5-writing-code -p "test_calculate.py"`

9. The following image shows what you get.

```
========================================================
FAIL: test_add (test_calculate.TestCalculate.test_add)
--------------------------------------------------------
Traceback (most recent call last):
  File "/Users/tomtaulli/Desktop/Projects/Code/AI-Assisted-Programming-Book/5-writing
-code/test_calculate.py", line 8, in test_add
    self.assertEqual(calculate('add', 2, 3), 6)
AssertionError: 5 != 6

--------------------------------------------------------
Ran 6 tests in 0.000s

FAILED (failures=1)
(base) tomtaulli@Mac AI-Assisted-Programming-Book % █
```

10. You can see that one of the tests failed. You can then go into your code and make the changes.

For this unit test, GitHub Copilot used the `unittest` library. Generally, it will select the most common one, based on its training data.

There is another way you can activate `/tests`. You select the code and right-click your mouse. A popup menu appears. You then select Copilot and click Generate Tests.

Suppose you have certain approaches to unit testing. Can you customize `/tests` for them? There is no built-in feature for this. But what you can do is have some of the sample test files loaded as tabs in your IDE. By doing this, GitHub will use this information as context when generating unit tests.

Custom Prompts

While the `/tests` slash command is convenient, it is not flexible. This is why you may want to write your own prompts for generating tests.

First, you might want to use a specific library. Here is a prompt:

> *Write unit tests using the pytest framework.*

If you do not know which one to use, you can ask GitHub Copilot for help. Here's a prompt:

> *For this code, what are the types of unit test frameworks I can use?*

You can follow this up with this prompt:

> *Which framework would you recommend?*

GitHub Copilot will provide an option and a rationale. You can also use the `/setupTests` slash command for this.

Then again, you can have GitHub Copilot write multiple tests and see which one looks the best:

> *For this code, write unit tests for the following frameworks: unittest, pytest, and nose2.*

When writing a prompt for unit tests, you can also ask GitHub to account for other details, such as edge cases you think are important, as well as testing for where data validation and exception handling are needed.

Let's see how you can use these factors. Suppose you are creating a shopping cart for an ecommerce site. It allows users to add, remove, and update items in their carts.

Here is a sample prompt:

> *Write a comprehensive suite of unit tests for the ShoppingCart class in Python. Ensure that the tests cover:*
>
> *Adding items to the cart, including duplicates.*
>
> *Removing items, ensuring correct quantities are updated.*
>
> *Handling edge cases like removing an item not in the cart or adding negative quantities.*
>
> *Verifying correct price calculations, including discount scenarios.*

Or another scenario is when you have an API endpoint that returns data based on a given user ID:

> *Create a robust set of unit tests for the* `get_user_data(user_id)` *function in Python. Cover different scenarios, including:*
>
> *Valid user ID returning correct user information.*
>
> *Invalid or nonexistent user ID returning appropriate errors.*
>
> *Handling requests when the database is down or unreachable.*
>
> *Ensuring security measures like authentication and rate limiting are properly enforced.*

With such prompts, you should get useful units tests. However, there can still be some gaps.

To help with this, you can use *coverage tools*. They help detect untested parts of your code. This is done by automated analysis for the execution of lines, branches, and functions. A coverage tool will provide a report, which has metrics such as:

- **Line coverage:** The percentage of executed lines of code.

- **Branch coverage:** The percentage of executed flow branches, such as `if/then/else` structures.

- **Function coverage:** The percentage of executed functions or methods.

Table 7.1 shows some of the popular coverage tools.

TABLE 7.1 Popular Coverage Tools

Tool	Language(s) Supported
JaCoCO	Java
Cobertura	Java
Jest	JavaScript, TypeScript
Istanbul (nyc)	JavaScript
Coverage.py	Python
pytest-cov	Python
Gcov	C, C++
BullseyeCoverage	C, C++
NCover	.NET (C#)

Integration Tests

This section looks at how to do integration tests using GitHub Copilot. Suppose you created this code:

```
import requests

class WeatherService:
    def __init__(self, api_key, base_url="https://api.weatherapi.com/v1"):
        self.api_key = api_key
        self.base_url = base_url

    def get_weather(self, city):
        endpoint = f"{self.base_url}/current.json"
        params = {"key": self.api_key, "q": city}
        response = requests.get(endpoint, params=params)
        response.raise_for_status()
        data = response.json()
        return data["current"]
```

This is a class, called `WeatherService`, that is an interface with an external weather API. It retrieves weather data for the specified city. The class uses the `requests` library, which uses the HTTP GET request for the API endpoint. This will include the parameters for the API key and city name. When the response is received, the class will process the JSON data to extract the weather information.

As mentioned earlier, it can be challenging to test a class or function that has a dependency, such as a call to an API. In other words, if there is an issue with the call, this may make it difficult to determine what the problem is. This can make the test unreliable.

Exercise 7.2 shows the steps for using GitHub Copilot for integration testing.

EXERCISE 7.2

Using Integration Testing with GitHub Copilot

1. Save the class as a file in your IDE.

2. At the top of the screen, click the GitHub Copilot icon and select Open Chat.

3. Highlight the function with your mouse or select the name of the file, which is under the Ask Copilot input box.

4. Enter the following prompt: *Generate integration tests for the* `get_weather` *method in the* `WeatherService` *class. Use the* `unittest` *framework and mock the* `requests` *.get method to simulate different API responses, including successful data retrieval, HTTP errors, and invalid JSON responses.*

5. The following image shows part of the integration tests.

```
1  import unittest
2  from unittest.mock import patch, Mock
3+ from test import WeatherService
4+
5+ class TestWeatherService(unittest.TestCase):
6+
7+     @patch('requests.get')
8+     def test_get_weather_success(self, mock_get):
9+         mock_response = Mock()
10+        expected_data = {"current": {"temp_c": 20}}
11+        mock_response.json.return_value = expected_data
12+        mock_response.raise_for_status = Mock()
13+        mock_get.return_value = mock_response
14+
15+        service = WeatherService(api_key="dummy_key")
16+        result = service.get_weather("London")
```

Let's take a deeper look at the generated code:

```
import unittest
from unittest.mock import patch, Mock
import requests
from weather_service import WeatherService
```

It imports `unittest`, which has the `unittest.mock` class. This provides tools for mocking objects for integration tests. It also imports the `WeatherService` class, which fetches the weather data.

Next, you create `TestWeatherService`, which inherits `unittest.TextCase`. It will contain methods for several tests. Here's one of them:

```
@patch('requests.get')
def test_get_weather_success(self, mock_get):
    mock_response = Mock()
    expected_data = {"current": {"temp_c": 20.0}}
    mock_response.json.return_value = expected_data
    mock_response.raise_for_status.return_value = None  # Corrected
    mock_get.return_value = mock_response

    service = WeatherService(api_key="fake_api_key")
    result = service.get_weather("London")
    self.assertEqual(result, expected_data["current"])
```

This mocks `requests.get` to simulate a successful API response. It will create a mock object, called `mock_response`, which has a predefined JSON payload called expected_data. You set mock_response.raise_for_status to do nothing. This shows there are no HTTP errors. You then assign mock_response as the return value of the mocked requests.get. After this, you create an instance of WeatherService and call get_weather. This will indicate that the returned data matches the expected data.

In some cases, you may not get a valid test. To address this, you can provide more details in your prompt, such as the inputs and outputs for the method or function.

Here is an example:

> *Generate integration tests for the get_weather method in the WeatherService class. Use the unittest framework and mock the requests.get method to simulate various API responses. Ensure that the tests cover:*
>
> *A successful API response with valid weather data.*
>
> *An HTTP error response, such as 404 Not Found.*
>
> *An invalid JSON response that raises a ValueError.*
>
> *A timeout exception when the API call exceeds the allowed time limit.*

Security Testing

Besides techniques like unit and integration testing, there is also security testing. This kind of testing evaluates the potential vulnerabilities in the code.

There are various approaches to security testing:

- **Scanning tools:** These are automated systems that detect security issues. This is done by comparing the results with a database of vulnerabilities.

- **Penetration testing or pen testing:** This is where realistic attacks are made against an application. This is usually done with ethical hackers.

- **Static application security testing (SAST):** You analyze the code without executing it, which helps detect security issues early in the development process.

- **Dynamic application security testing (DAST):** This is where you evaluate the security vulnerabilities as you run the application.

- **Security audits:** These are intensive evaluations of the software's security by a third party. They not only review the code but also the policies and procedures.

Unit testing with GitHub Copilot can help with security testing. The tests can mitigate issues, such as by spotting problems with potential inputs and outputs. For example, it can make tests for error handling, null values, or expected values.

You can also use GitHub Copilot as a basic security scanner. For example, suppose you have the following JavaScript code:

```javascript
function displayUserComment(comment) {
  const commentSection = document.getElementById('comments');
```

```
  const p = document.createElement('p');
  p.textContent = comment;
  commentSection.appendChild(p);
}
```

Exercise 7.3 shows how to evaluate this code using GitHub Copilot.

EXERCISE 7.3

Using GitHub Copilot for Security Scanning

1. Save the class as a file in your IDE.

2. At the top of the screen, click the GitHub Copilot icon and select Open Chat.

3. Highlight the function with your mouse or select the name of the file, which is under the Ask Copilot input box.

4. Enter the following prompt: *Analyze this code for potential security vulnerabilities and suggest fixes.*

5. GitHub identifies that this code could lead to a cross-site scripting (XSS) attack if a user submits a comment using JavaScript code.

6. The following image shows the suggested code that is more secure, which uses a library called DOMPurify.

```
Here is the revised code with DOMPurify:

function displayUserComment(comment) {
  const commentSection = document.getElementById('comment
  const p = document.createElement('p');

  // Sanitize the comment to prevent XSS attacks
  const sanitizedComment = DOMPurify.sanitize(comment);

  p.textContent = sanitizedComment;
  commentSection.appendChild(p);
}
```

However, you should not rely only on GitHub Copilot for security scanning. It is a good idea to use a specialized tool like SonarQube or Veracode.

The remaining part of this chapter focuses on the next domain for the exam: privacy.

Privacy Fundamentals

Since its early days, privacy has been a major priority for GitHub. The company has an extensive General Privacy Statement that details how information is collected, processed, protected, and shared. There is also a comprehensive document for legal requests of user data.

Privacy has been a key factor for GitHub's strong growth. The reason is that users must have trust in placing their valuable code into the platform. GitHub is the world's largest repository and is a must-have for millions of developers.

With the growth of AI, GitHub has become an important source of training data for advanced models. Yet this has raised important questions about privacy. Should this code be used? What are the developer's rights? What about users who enter information into the models, such as with GitHub Copilot? How is this information used? Who owns it?

GitHub has recognized the privacy issues and has been proactive in updating their methods, such as with updates to the privacy statement. It has done this by abiding by the following principle[2]:

"At GitHub, we recognize that user privacy is not just a matter of policy but a fundamental human right. GitHub is committed to protecting this right by embedding privacy into its operations and products."

Along with this, GitHub has set forth three core tenants:

- **Respect for user privacy:** GitHub treats your data with utmost care and integrity. The company's teams are trained to understand the best practices and standards for protecting user information.

- **Transparency and control:** As much as it can, GitHub is open with its policies. You can find this at its Trust Center at `https://github.com/trust-center/privacy`. In terms of control, GitHub believes that users own their data and the code generated from the AI system.

- **Privacy by design:** For every step of development, there is a focus on privacy.

GitHub's focus on privacy is not only for its own services. This extends to data protection with third parties, such as partners. They must comply with the GitHub Data Processing Agreement (DPA), which is a set of requirements and obligations for data privacy and security.

When it comes to data collection, GitHub's approach is to collect only what's necessary. Through the settings in your account, you can view and update how data is controlled. First, you can make your profile and email private. You can see how to do this in Exercise 7.4.

EXERCISE 7.4

Setting Privacy Settings in GitHub Copilot

1. In the upper-right corner of `GitHub.com`, click your profile photo.

2. Select Settings.

3. You will see the following screen.

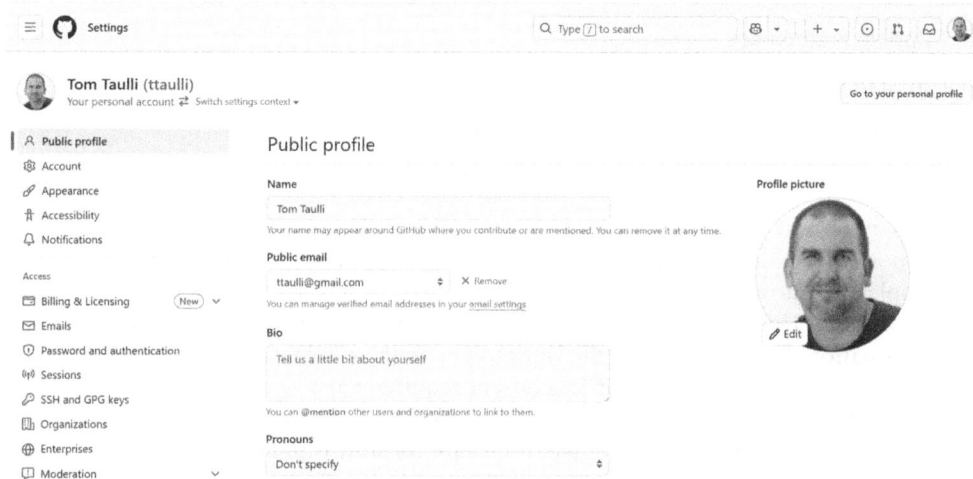

4. To make your profile private, select Make Profile Private and Hide Activity.

5. Click Update Preferences.

6. If you want to make your email private, select Emails from the sidebar. This is under the Access section.

7. Select Keep My Email Address Private. GitHub will then set it to an email like this: `738833+janedoe@users.noreply.github.com`. This will be used when performing Git operations, such as for edits and merges.

8. Another privacy feature is the ability to completely delete an account. In the sidebar, select Account.

9. At the bottom of the screen, click Delete Your Account. You then need to confirm this action.

GitHub provides for data portability. This allows you to archive your profile information, repositories, issues, and pull requests. Exercise 7.5 shows how to do this.

EXERCISE 7.5

Exporting GitHub Data

1. In the upper-right corner of `GitHub.com`, click your profile photo.

2. Select Settings.

3. Click Account.

4. To make your profile private, select Make Profile Private and Hide Activity.

5. Click Update Preferences.

6. Choose Start Export.

7. You will receive an email when the export is finished.

It's important to note that data privacy is not monolithic. It depends on a complex set of laws, regulations and standards. This can also vary by country or state.

For example, the European Union's General Data Protection Regulation (GDPR) is a comprehensive data protection law. It applies in many situations, such as when processing personal information. EU citizens have the right to access their data, correct inaccuracies, and transfer their data. There are also strict consent requirements.

Then there is California's Consumer Privacy Act (CCPA). This also provides extensive protections for personal data. They mandate disclosure for how organizations collect, disclose, and sell data. Residents also have the right to delete their data and to opt out of the sale of their personal information.

Privacy for Versions of GitHub Copilot

In Chapter 3, you saw that the different versions of GitHub Copilot come with many features. The same goes for privacy. However, the GitHub version does not categorize for this. Table 7.2 shows the different versions and their privacy features.

As you can see, the features are offered in the Business and Enterprise editions. This is not to imply that the lower versions deserve less protection. Rather, it is based on needs. For teams and larger organizations, privacy requirements can be much more stringent. For example, a healthcare or financial services organization will be under considerable regulatory and legal oversight. But if you are a solo developer creating a program to help with organizing recipes, it would be overly burdensome to add a high level of privacy protection.

The next few sections take a further look at these options. The exception is the topic of data retention and IP protection, which is covered in Chapter 4.

TABLE 7.2   Privacy Features in GitHub Copilot

Privacy Feature	Free	Individual (Pro)	Business	Enterprise
Organization-wide policy management			X	X
Exclusion of files			X	X
Audit logs			X	X
Blocking of suggestions matching public code			X	X
Zero data retention for code snippets and usage telemetry			X	X
IP protection			X	X

Organization-Wide Policy Management Exclusion of Files

When you have an organization setup in GitHub, you have the following available with GitHub Copilot:

- **Audit logs:** These monitor and track the usage of GitHub Copilot within an organization.

- **Content exclusions:** You can exclude repositories and files from being used as training for GitHub Copilot's AI models or generating suggestions.

- **Policy management:** An administrator can set policies for how GitHub Copilot is used for an organization, such as to enable or disable the tools for certain teams or projects.

- **GitHub Copilot REST API:** You can create programs that manage subscriptions, such as when assigning or revoking licenses.

I addressed these topics in the book previously; however, these sections cover more details for audit logs, content exclusions, and policy management.

Audit Logs

For GitHub Copilot, there are 18 events for audit logs. Table 7.3 shows some of them.

TABLE 7.3   GitHub Copilot Audit Log Events

Action	Description
copilot.cfb_seat_assignment_created	A seat was assigned to a user.
copilot.cfb_seat_assignment_deleted	A seat for a user was deleted.
copilot.cfb_seat_assignment_updated	A seat assignment was updated.
copilot.cfb_subscription_created	A new subscription to GitHub Copilot was created.
copilot.cfb_subscription_deleted	An existing subscription to GitHub Copilot was deleted.
copilot.cfb_subscription_updated	An existing GitHub Copilot subscription was updated.

The transparency of audit logs can help with privacy. You can use them to monitor logins, data access, and modifications. This can help detect unauthorized or suspicious activities, which could lead to privacy breaches.

The audit logs may also serve as evidence for compliance with privacy regulations and laws. Keep in mind that there are often recordkeeping and monitoring requirements.

However, if there is a security breach, the audit logs can help provide a record of what led up to and followed the incidence. This can help with the investigation to find the root cause of the compromise.

Finally, the fact that there are audit logs can act as a deterrent. Employees and contractors may be less inclined to engage in unauthorized activities.

Content Exclusions

You can configure GitHub Copilot to exclude certain content from being used in code completion suggestions. This can be helpful with privacy. You can make sure that data like API keys, passwords, personal user information, and other critical data is not available for Copilot to index on its servers.

This is what you can exclude:

- **Specific files:** You can exclude a file by specifying the path, such as /config/ settings.yaml.

- **Files by name:** If you want to exclude specific files for the repository, you specify the name of the file, such as credentials.json.

- **Files by pattern:** You can exclude files according to a pattern. Here are examples: `config.*` and `*.bak`.
- **Directories:** To exclude all files in a directory and its subdirectories, you use the name of the directory, such as `/logs/**`.

While there are clear benefits for privacy and security, there are downsides for content exclusions. They reduce the context for GitHub Copilot to generate useful responses. For example, suppose you are writing a financial application that has a `config/database .yaml` file. You exclude this for GitHub Copilot. However, let's say you write a function called `fetch_transactions(start_date,end_date)`, which needs to establish a database connection to write effective SQL queries. In this case, the response from GitHub Copilot will likely not be useful or accurate. You will have to manually write the code.

What this means is that there is a trade-off with privacy and functionality. This is a judgment call based on the sensitivity of the information, the compliance requirements, and the performance of GitHub Copilot.

This is why you might want more granular exclusions. Instead of excluding file patterns or directories, you can focus on specific files. There should also be regular reviews for updates on the exclusions to make sure they are meeting the needs of the organization.

When you set up content exclusions, they may not necessarily be applied. One reason is that they can take up to 30 minutes to take effect in the IDE. But a solution is to restart the IDE, which will force the update.

Another reason is the scope of the content exclusion. For example, suppose you have sensitive information in the `config.yaml` file. For the organization level, you exclude such files for all the repositories. But suppose an administrator does not know this and they remove the content exclusion in a specific repository. The result is that there is a conflict between the organization and repository. This can lead to unexpected results, in terms of the use of the file. This is why it is important to be consistent with the exclusion settings for the organization and individual repositories.

Policy Management

You can carry out your organization's policies for GitHub Copilot by making changes to the configuration file for your IDE. This allows you to make customizations to the different capabilities of GitHub Copilot.

Table 7.4 shows this for Chat.

This information is stored in `settings.json`. If you want to allow GitHub Copilot to use all languages except YAML and plaintext, you can add this:

```
{
  "github.copilot.enable": {
    "*": true,
    "yaml": false,
    "plaintext": false
  }
}
```

TABLE 7.4   Configuration for GitHub Copilot Chat

Feature	Description
`github.copilot.chat.followUps`	Determines whether GitHub Copilot should suggest follow-up queries in Chat.
`github.copilot.chat.localeOverride`	Provides a locale that GitHub Copilot should respond with, such as English or German.
`chat.editor.fontFamily`	Font family for the Chat code.
`chat.editor.wordWrap`	Sets the line wrapping.
`chat.implicitContext.enabled`	Sets whether the active editor should be added as context to the Chat prompt by default.
`github.copilot.chat.terminalChatLocation`	Determines where Chat questions from the terminal should be opened.

The * character means that the configuration is globally set for all languages. But then `yaml` and `plaintext` are set to `false`.

You can also make this change using the Settings function in VS Code. Exercise 7.6 shows the steps for this.

EXERCISE 7.6

Updating the Configuration of GitHub Copilot in VS Code

1. At the bottom left of the screen of VS Code, click the gear icon.

2. Select Settings.

3. Enter the following in the search box at the top: *copilot*.

4. You will see the following screen.

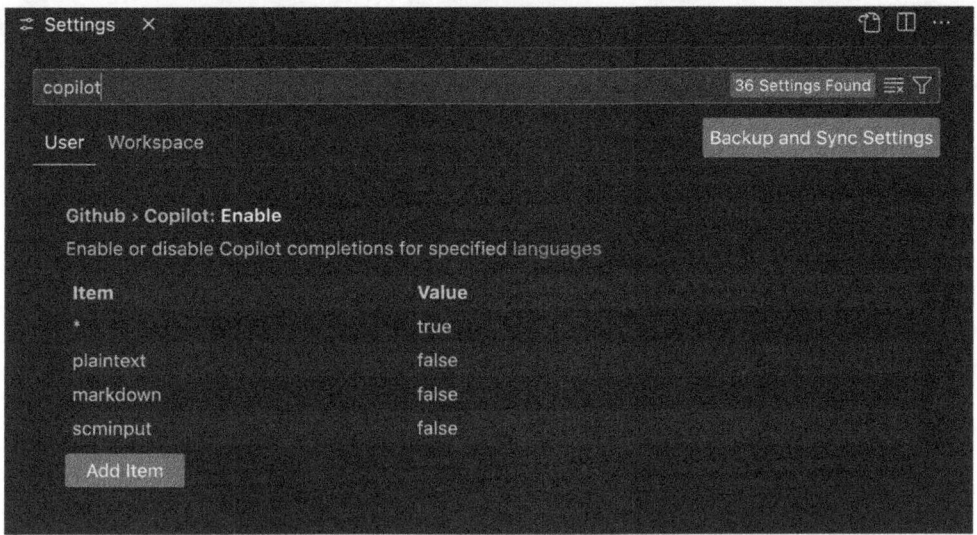

5. By default, GitHub Copilot will use all languages for completions. But you can disable those listed by hovering your mouse over the right side of the item and selecting the pencil icon. You can then turn the value to true.

6. At the top of the screen, there are tabs for User and Workspace. This means you can have the updates apply to a particular user account or for a project.

7. As you scroll down the screen, you will see many other options you can easily change for the configuration file. There are over 30.

Block Suggestions Matching Public Code

Chapter 3 discussed the public code filter, which is also referred to as the duplication detector filter. It identifies generated code in public repositories. This is a way to mitigate the potential for intellectual property violations. GitHub also provides IP indemnity, which is a legal defense for certain litigation.

On GitHub.com, you can configure the duplication detector filter. Exercise 7.7 shows how to do this.

EXERCISE 7.7

Updating the Duplication Detector on GitHub.com

1. Click your photo on the top right of the screen on GitHub.com.

2. Select Your Copilot.

3. On the left sidebar, click Copilot.

4. Scroll down until you see this: Suggestions matching public code (duplication detection filter).

5. If you select Blocked, this means GitHub Copilot will not show suggestions matching public code.

6. Below this, you will see: Allow GitHub to use my data for product improvements. This is selected true as a default. This means that GitHub, as well as its affiliates and third parties, can use your data for making the product better. The data includes prompts, suggestions, and code snippets.

Troubleshooting

If GitHub Copilot is not providing responses for code suggestions, the problem could be that the extension is not current. The update process is different in terms of the IDE you use. Exercise 7.8 shows the process for VS Code.

EXERCISE 7.8

Updating the GitHub Copilot Extension

1. Click the Extensions icon on the Activity bar on the left side of VS Code's screen. You can also use Ctrl+Shift+X for Windows and Cmd+Shift+X for macOS.

2. Search for the GitHub Copilot Extension. You can type **GitHub Copilot** in the search box.

3. You will see the following screen.

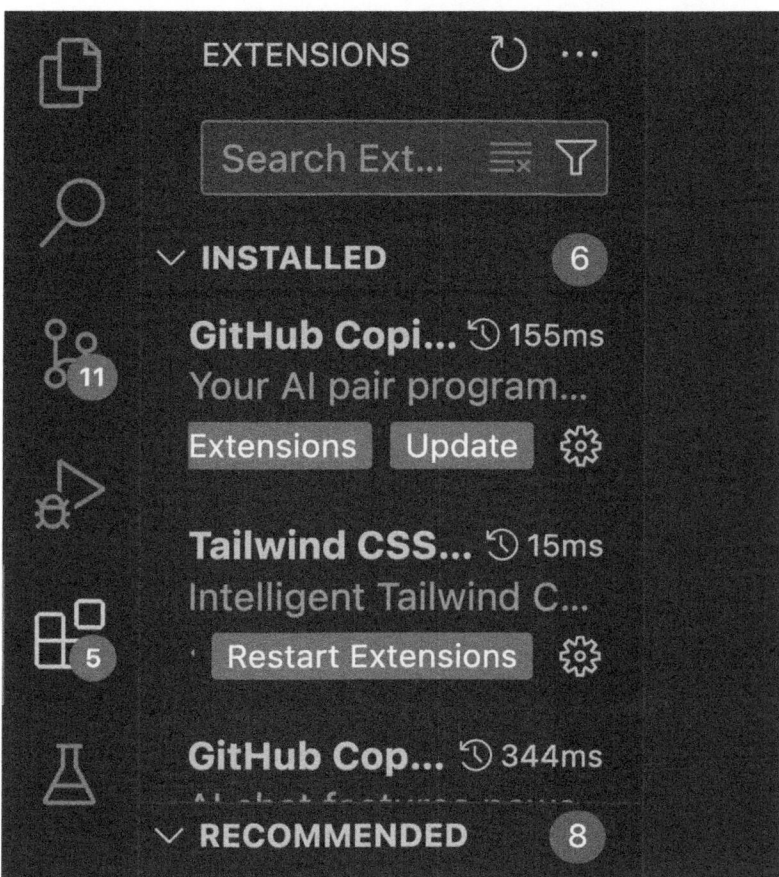

4. Click the Update button.

5. Click the Reload button.

Finally, when using GitHub Copilot, you may not want to have it generate automatic code suggestions when you are working in the IDE. You can turn off this feature, which depends on your IDE. With VS Code, you add this to the settings.json file:

```
"editor.inlineSuggest.enabled": false
```

GitHub Advanced Security

GitHub Advanced Security (GHAS) is a suite of security solutions, such as for scanning, secret scanning, and dependency reviews. Many of the features are free for public repositories, but there is a subscription required for private repositories.

GHAS also has the Copilot Autofix feature. This leverages AI to analyze issues detected during code scanning and suggests fixes. They are presented in a pull request, which allows for a seamless developer experience.

Summary

This chapter covered the last two domains on the exam. The first one was about testing with GitHub Copilot. You got an overview of the fundamentals and the different approaches. You then saw some demos of how to use unit testing and integration testing with GitHub Copilot. This also included best practices, as well as using the /tests slash command and custom prompts.

The next domain was about privacy and content exclusions. You first looked at GitHub's approach to privacy and how it is a core value. You then saw how to use the different privacy features, such as exporting data, excluding files, using audit logs, and working with policy management.

Exam Essentials

Understand how GitHub Copilot improves software testing. GitHub Copilot streamlines unit and integration testing. It will create the boilerplate code for the testing, which will be customized based on the function or block of code. You can also do this using a TDD workflow, allowing you to write tests before implementation. This can help improve reliability.

Learn how to use GitHub Copilot for unit testing. GitHub can create unit tests for common use cases, edge cases, and error conditions. The /tests slash command allows you to do this quickly. But you can also use custom prompts, such as by specifying the testing framework and setting forth what you want tested.

Understand integration testing with GitHub Copilot. GitHub Copilot can create integration tests that use mocks for external dependencies like APIs. You should know how to refine these tests for certain kinds of responses.

Know about how to use GitHub Copilot for security testing. You can use GitHub Copilot to scan security vulnerabilities, such as SQL injection and cross-site scripting (XSS).

This is done by using prompts. GitHub Copilot will not only spot the security issues but also suggest fixes.

Understand privacy settings and content exclusions.   You should know that GitHub Copilot can be configured to exclude files. This means that sensitive or proprietary data will not be used for suggestions. You should also understand that this can be done at an organizational level and for specified repositories. But you need to be careful. You do not want these to conflict. Otherwise, data may be exposed. You should also know that you can enable and disable automatic suggestions.

Know about troubleshooting Copilot issues.   In some cases, Copilot may not generate suggestions. You should know how to resolve this, such as by updating the Copilot extension, ensuring the correct settings are enabled, and troubleshooting context exclusions.

Review Questions

1. Which of the following best describes the role of software testing in the Software Development Life Cycle (SDLC)?
   A. Software testing is only done when the code has been completely debugged.
   B. Software testing verifies if an application does what it is intended to do.
   C. Software testing only involves automated methods.
   D. Software testing is the same as Quality Assurance (QA).

2. What is the role of unit testing in software development?
   A. To evaluate the overall functionality of a software project
   B. To test individual functional units of the codebase in isolation
   C. To ensure the software meets customer requirements before it goes into production
   D. To identify performance issues with the software

3. What is a drawback of unit testing?
   A. It cannot be used with test-driven development (TDD).
   B. It is not automated.
   C. It is not available in GitHub Copilot.
   D. It does not allow for testing how various units of software interact with each other.

4. When writing unit tests, which is not a best practice?
   A. Having each test focus on a single expected outcome
   B. Trying to anticipate potential pathways for the code
   C. Writing tests for at least two functions
   D. Keeping tests independent from one another

5. What best describes test-driven development (TDD) when using unit testing?
   A. Tests are written before the code is implemented.
   B. TDD is only for integration testing.
   C. TDD is a manual approach to testing.
   D. TDD is for security scanning.

6. Why should unit tests be independent from one another?
   A. It increases the speed of the testing.
   B. It ensures one failed test does not affect the outcomes of other tests.
   C. It means there is no need for automated tools.
   D. It means that all test cases will pass on the first attempt.

7. What is the purpose of integration testing?

   A. To test separate functional units of the codebase in isolation

   B. To focus only on debugging the code

   C. To create tests before writing the code

   D. To evaluate the interactions between different components of the code

8. Which integration testing technique begins by testing the core modules and then moves downward to other ones?

   A. Bottom-up integration testing

   B. Exploratory integration testing

   C. Top-down integration testing

   D. Big-bang integration testing

9. What is an advantage of using GitHub Copilot for unit testing?

   A. It covers all edge cases available.

   B. It generates boilerplate unit test code.

   C. It automatically fixes failed tests.

   D. It eliminates the need for manual test reviews.

10. Which command will generate unit tests in GitHub Copilot?

   A. `/tests`

   B. `/setupTests`

   C. `/unittests`

   D. `/units`

11. What is a drawback when using the `/tests` slash command in GitHub Copilot?

   A. It cannot generate tests for functions that include mathematical calculations.

   B. It does not allow customization of the generated test framework or test structure.

   C. It only supports JavaScript and Python for creating unit tests.

   D. It does not work with testing frameworks like pytest or unittest.

12. What is a best practice when using GitHub Copilot to generate unit tests?

   A. Run code coverage tools to identify untested parts of the code.

   B. Avoid using custom prompts.

   C. Always specify the testing framework.

   D. Identify all the edge cases.

13. Why should you use mocks for external API calls when writing integration tests for a function?

    A. To avoid making real API calls and ensuring tests run consistently

    B. To increase the speed of the tests

    C. To automatically fix bugs in the API

    D. To allow direct modification of API responses in production

14. What is a best practice for generating integration tests for API calls using GitHub Copilot?

    A. Allow GitHub Copilot to generate tests without reviewing them.

    B. Use specific prompts to ensure edge cases like timeouts and invalid JSON responses are tested.

    C. Always make real API calls to get the most accurate test results.

    D. Avoid testing for HTTP errors, as they rarely occur in production.

15. Which is not one of GitHub's core privacy principles?

    A. Respect for user privacy

    B. Transparency and control

    C. Privacy by design

    D. Complete anonymity for all users

16. How does GitHub allow users to manage their privacy settings?

    A. By providing options to make their profile and email private

    B. By preventing users from exporting their data

    C. By requiring all repositories to be private

    D. By requiring an Enterprise plan

17. Which version of GitHub Copilot provides organization-wide policy management and file exclusion?

    A. Free and Individual (Pro)

    B. Business and Enterprise

    C. Individual (Pro) and Business

    D. All versions of GitHub Copilot

18. Which of the following privacy features are available only in the Business and Enterprise editions of GitHub Copilot?

    A. Audit logs

    B. Exclusion of files

    C. Blocking of suggestions matching public code

    D. All of the above

19. What is a reason for configuring content exclusions in GitHub Copilot?

    A. To speed up Copilot's response time when generating code

    B. To prevent sensitive data like API keys and passwords from being used in code suggestions

    C. To allow Copilot to generate more accurate responses by accessing all repository files

    D. To disable GitHub Copilot for a repository

20. Which of the following steps can help resolve issues if GitHub Copilot is not providing code suggestions?

    A. Restarting the IDE and checking for Copilot extension updates

    B. Deleting the configuration files in the repository

    C. Reinstalling your IDE

    D. Configuring the settings in `GitHub.com`

Notes

1. TechTarget (August 2022). Software Testing. https://www.techtarget.com/whatis/definition/software-testing (accessed 10 March 2025).

2. https://github.com/trust-center/privacy

Appendix

Answers to Review Questions

Chapter 1: The Fundamentals of AI and Its Responsible Use

1.   C. AI coding systems have revolutionized software development. But they have clear drawbacks too. These tools can generate code with security vulnerabilities like SQL injections or buffer overflows. They may also create bloated code. Because of the issues, developers should always review code generated by AI coding systems.

2.   B. Supervised learning is a machine learning technique that uses labeled data. This means that each training example includes both input data and the correct output. This allows an algorithm to learn from the dataset by mapping the inputs to the outputs.

3.   A. The SWE-bench (Software Engineering Benchmark) is tailored for evaluating the performance of AI models for software development. The other benchmarks mentioned in the answers are for other use cases. For example, ImageNet is for computer vision and the BERTScore is for language understanding. As for the Turing test, it is not a benchmark. It is instead a general test to gauge if a system is AI.

4.   B. Generally, AI-generated code is secure. But there can still be vulnerabilities. Examples include SQL injections, buffer overflows, and cross-site scripting threats. The reason for these dangers is that the underlying training data may suffer from insecure practices. As a result, developers should do a security review of their AI-generated code.

5.   C. Generally, a recommendation system will use unsupervised learning. This would include clustering algorithms. For example, they would find patterns in the unlabeled data.

6.   B. Sometimes AI-generated code can be bloated. It could have unnecessary steps, inconsistent variables names, and redundant logic or functions. Bloated code can be difficult to maintain and update. This is why there needs to be refactoring of AI-generated code.

7.   C. A major limitation of AI models is that they can create hallucinations. These are the result of poor quality of the dataset and the probabilistic nature of the transformer model. Sometimes, the code is incorrect. In other cases, it may work but not do what was intended.

8.   B. Reinforcement learning is a machine learning (ML) technique. It is where a system learns by interacting with an environment. With an AI model for a self-driving car, it can improve its navigation by getting rewarded for positive results, like avoiding obstacles or staying on the right side of the road. By the same token, there can penalties for negative results like deviating from a lane.

9.   A. Multimodel AI coding systems give users the option to choose from multiple AI models, such as OpenAI's GPT, Anthropic's Claude, and Google's Gemini. Different models have varying strengths in code generation, reasoning, and problem-solving. A developer can experiment with the models to see which ones work for a particular task. They can also use benchmarks to evaluate the AI models.

10. A. Fine-tuning an LLM involves modifying the model's parameters. This is done by training it on a new dataset. However, this is a complicated process that requires skilled data scientists. RAG, on the other hand, is a much simpler process. It uses a search algorithm that is connected to a dataset.

11. B. Generative AI models can generate hallucinations. This is where the information may seem correct but is actually misleading or false.

12. A. If an AI model is trained on biased dataset, then this can lead to unintentional discrimination. With fairness—which is a principle of responsible AI—this can be identified and mitigated.

13. B. AI models can reflect biases in their training datasets. But there are ways to handle this, such as with bias detection tools and retraining the model with diverse and representative data.

14. B. AI ethics teams are key for monitoring and mitigating ethical risks. They help detect bias and privacy issues. They should also have periodic audits to provide for responsible AI.

15. B. AI in financial in the financial services industry is highly regulated. When it uses this technology, it needs to meet rigorous legal, ethical, and compliance requirements. There should also be periodic audits.

16. B. AI models trained on user data can sometimes generate responses that unintentionally expose personal or confidential information. This is due to the complex nature of the underlying AI algorithms. This why it's important to implement strong privacy policies.

17. A. AI systems should undergo extensive testing and monitoring. This will help ensure reliability. This is especially important for critical applications, such as for finance and healthcare.

18. D. Inclusiveness ensures that AI systems are designed to be accessible and beneficial for all. This includes individuals with disabilities.

19. C. Transparency helps to improve trust in AI systems. This is done by making the decision-making processes understandable and explainable to users.

20. B. Accountability ensures AI systems operate responsibly. For this, it's important to set forth clear policies with ethical guidelines.

Chapter 2: Introduction to GitHub Copilot

1. C. GitHub Copilot provides real-time code suggestions based on the context. It does not replace manual testing, version control, or perform automatic refactoring without input.

2. B. Various studies highlight that GitHub Copilot helps developers complete tasks faster. This is especially true for tasks that are repetitive and tedious. This means developers have more time to focus on problem solving.

3. D. Copilot Enterprise includes advanced security, compliance features, and integration with enterprise-grade environments. This is the best fit for large organizations.

4. B. GitHub Copilot Chat helps developers by offering context-aware suggestions, explanations, and debugging support. This helps improve the efficiency of coding workflows.

5. B. GitHub Copilot automatically suggests inline completions when developers type comments or begin a code snippet. This helps make coding faster and more efficient.

6. A. GitHub Copilot supports multiple programming languages. As a result, it can help with both frontend and backend development. But this does not replace manual configuration or guarantee security.

7. B. GitHub Copilot can generate code in a requested language and provide explanations. This makes it an effective tool for learning new programming concepts.

8. C. While GitHub Copilot helps to improve productivity, developers must manually validate generated code to ensure it meets functional and security requirements.

9. A. To use GitHub Copilot in the CLI, developers must install the GitHub CLI, authenticate their GitHub account, and enable the Copilot extension.

10. B. Providing clear prompts helps GitHub Copilot generate more accurate and relevant responses.

11. B. The /test slash command prompts GitHub Copilot to generate test cases for the given code.

12. A. Slash commands like /test and /fix help developers quickly perform tasks like generating test cases and debugging.

13. B. To use GitHub Copilot in VS Code, developers must first install the extension from the VS Code Marketplace.

14. B. GitHub Copilot generates code based on training data. While it can improve productivity, it may also introduce security vulnerabilities that require manual review.

15. A. Providing clear comments and structure helps GitHub Copilot generate more relevant and high-quality code suggestions.

16. B. The `gh copilot chat` command enables GitHub Copilot Chat in the CLI. This allows developers to use the AI assistant from the terminal.

17. A. The `gh copilot explain` command allows GitHub Copilot to provide explanations for error messages in the terminal.

18. A. Inline chat provides contextual AI assistance directly within the IDE. This allows developers to stay in the flow.

19. D. GitHub Copilot Edits enables developers to make AI-powered modifications across multiple files at once. This can greatly increase productivity.

20. A. The *explain* command in GitHub Copilot Chat provides insights into how a function works.

Chapter 3: Differences in GitHub Copilot Versions

1. C. Knowledge bases are a feature unique to GitHub Copilot Enterprise. They help improve code quality, consistency, and efficiency by storing design patterns, best practices, and reusable code snippets. The other options are available in lower-tier versions as well.

2. A. GitHub Copilot Business includes centralized billing. This helps streamline payment management for organizations. The Individual version, on the other hand, is meant for personal use, with separate billing for each user.

3. B. Custom models allow organizations to fine-tune the LLM to their specific coding standards, patterns, and practices. This improves relevance and productivity.

4. B. GitHub Copilot generates pull request summaries by analyzing the changes made in the pull request and creating a natural language summary. This helps reviewers understand the modifications.

5. C. Audit logs in GitHub Copilot Business provide a chronological record of activities and changes to settings. This helps with compliance, security, and accountability.

6. B. Knowledge bases help improve code quality by embedding shared best practices, design patterns, and reusable code snippets. They ensure consistency across projects and teams.

7. C. Organization-wide policy management is supported in GitHub Copilot Business and Enterprise. This allows organizations to enforce consistent policies across all users.

8. B. Custom models are exclusive to GitHub Copilot Enterprise. They allow organizations to fine-tune AI models to their specific coding practices.

9. D. Organization administrators can exclude specific files from being accessed by GitHub Copilot by adding the file paths to the organization's Copilot settings. This prevents Copilot from using the content for code suggestions.

10. B. Knowledge bases are exclusive to GitHub Copilot Enterprise. They provide advanced customization and consistency by storing best practices, design patterns, and reusable code snippets.

11. C. IP indemnity is provided in GitHub Copilot Business and Enterprise versions. It provides legal protection against intellectual property claims related to AI-generated code.

12. B. The GitHub REST API allows administrators to automate seat assignments, manage subscriptions, and track usage metrics in Copilot Business.

13. C. The public code filter checks AI-generated code against public repositories to avoid potential intellectual property violations by identifying matches and displaying relevant licenses.

14. A. The GitHub Copilot REST API is used for automating subscription management tasks such as assigning and revoking seats, as well as for retrieving usage metrics.

15. C. Organization-wide content exclusions are available in both Business and Enterprise versions. They allow administrators to restrict Copilot's access to specific files for privacy and compliance.

16. C. GitHub Copilot Business allows administrators to filter audit log events by type, date, and user actions. This makes it easier to track policy changes and activities.

17. B. Pull request summaries in GitHub Copilot provide a natural language overview of code changes. They help reviewers understand modifications more efficiently.

18. D. Centralized billing allows organizations to manage payments for all team members under a single account. This helps simplify financial administration.

19. B. Organization-wide content exclusions allow administrators to prevent specific files from being accessed or analyzed by GitHub Copilot. This helps organizations maintain data privacy and compliance with regulations.

20. A. In GitHub Copilot Enterprise, knowledge bases are created by storing relevant markdown files, such as code snippets, best practices, and design patterns, in selected repositories. These are indexed and used to enhance code completion and review.

Chapter 4: The Role of Data

1. C. GitHub Copilot processes user input for generating suggestions but does not store it permanently. However, a user can opt in for this. In this case, the data will be used to improve existing models.

2. B. The proxy service helps prevent sensitive data from being exposed before it reaches the AI model.

3. A. Copilot prioritizes commonly seen code patterns. This means that the suggestions can be influenced by older or widely used examples.

4. A. GitHub Copilot applies a code referencing filter to notify users. This detects whether the suggested code closely matches publicly available code.

5. A. GitHub Copilot Chat often processes more complex queries, such as debugging or documentation generation, which usually require more time.

6. D. Copilot improves accuracy by using in-file context, user comments, and the cursor's location to generate relevant suggestions.

7. C. GitHub Copilot struggles with precise mathematical calculations because it lacks an internal computation engine.

8. A. AI models rely on preexisting datasets, and if they are not frequently updated, they may lack knowledge of newer technologies, techniques, or best practices.

9. C. GitHub Copilot processes user inputs in real-time but does not store them permanently. This helps ensure user privacy.

10. A. GitHub Copilot includes a code referencing filter to notify users when generated code closely resembles public repository content.

11. D. GitHub Copilot Chat is useful for debugging, generating documentation, and providing detailed code explanations beyond simple code completion.

12. C. GitHub Copilot has a fixed context window. This means it can only analyze a portion of the surrounding code before generating a response. This can potentially lead to less effective code suggestions.

13. A. Post-processing ensures that GitHub Copilot's suggestions are properly formatted and free from redundant or syntactically incorrect elements.

14. B. GitHub Copilot relies on cloud-based AI models and cannot operate in environments that lack external network access.

15. B. High-quality data helps AI models make accurate predictions and reduces bias. This helps ensure more reliable outputs.

16. A. Copilot focuses on the active file to generate the most contextually relevant code completions.

17. B. Disabling telemetry prevents GitHub from collecting user activity data for performance analysis and product improvement.

18. D. Metadata includes information like file paths and programming languages. This helps GitHub Copilot generate suggestions that fit the user's project.

19. A. AI-generated code may introduce security risks if it suggests insecure coding practices.

20. D. GitHub Copilot uses optimized cloud resources to ensure fast response times for code completions.

Chapter 5: Prompt Crafting and Engineering

1. C. Prompt engineering is about writing clear instructions for the large language model. It helps provide a guide for creating more accurate and relevant responses.

2. C. The four parts of a prompt are the context, instructions, input of content, and format. Code execution is something that GitHub Copilot cannot do.

3. B. Writing a good prompt is about balancing clarity and sufficient detail. But if there it is too long, the large language model may get "lost in the middle," ignoring or misinterpreting information details.

4. A. With few-shot learning, you will include a few examples of the types of responses you want. This helps the large language model to better understand the patterns so as to generate higher quality responses.

5. B. CoT prompting is about using multiple prompts. They are broken down into logical steps. With each one, the focus is on the reasoning of the large language model.

6. D. Since GitHub is open with what you can input as a prompt, there is a risk that you could expose sensitive data, such as names, addresses, and account numbers. You should either avoid this or anonymize the data.

7. B. Even though GitHub Copilot is trained on huge amounts of data, there are still gaps. This is especially the case with more obscure programming languages.

8. C. Agentic AI engages in multi-step reasoning. Much of this will be done autonomously. This means that there will be less detailed prompts, such as in specifying steps or how to approach a task. The agentic AI will use its own reasoning and planning capabilities for this.

9. D. GitHub Copilot does not support a specific number of languages. But it does support a large number of them. These languages are part of the massive training dataset for the large language model.

10. B. Zero-short learning is when you prompt GitHub Copilot without using examples. It's generally the most common way to interact with this tool. But with few-shot learning, you can provide several examples to provide a guide for the large language model to generate better responses.

11. B. LLMs can translate many languages because of the vast dataset. But it may not necessarily capture idiomatic expressions and cultural nuances. This can lead to a situation where you offend or confuse users.

12. A. This is a delimiter, which separates the instructions from the content. For example, this could be when you summarize information.

13. C. With leading words, you can help guide the large language model. This may actually be one or two words, such as a command like CREATE TABLE.

14. D. Being specific with the type of response can be helpful in mitigating the issues with hallucinations. There are fewer opportunities for the large language model to stray.

15. B. This is used to help generate better responses, as well as the cursor position and code edits.

16. A. This prompt is too vague. For example, it should specify what the form is for as well as the fields. It could be something like: *Create a form for a login that has a field for a username and password.*

17. D. CoT prompting is effective with complex problem solving, which can lead to higher quality responses. However, the extra processing means that the responses can be slower.

18. B. Generally, it's better to have one instruction or task for a prompt. This lessens the possibility of GitHub Copilot emphasizing one over the other.

19. C. An example of specifying a role is to start a prompt with something like, *You are an expert at programming Python.* This provides the LLM with more context to generate a more relevant response.

20. C. While these models all use the core transformer model, there are variations on the implementation. The datasets are also different.

Chapter 6: Developer Use Cases for GitHub Copilot

1. C. You can prompt GitHub Copilot to learn a language. But the explanations can be personalized, based on your experience and use cases.

2. B. GitHub Copilot will not create files. You will need to copy and paste the generated code and place it in a file that you created on your system.

3. D. With GitHub Copilot, you can specify the files of an API to generate documentation. It can also be done in different formats, like Markdown.

4. A. GitHub Copilot is particularly good with logic errors, as the LLM can detect complex patterns. The other errors mentioned in the question are usually better handled by a compiler.

5. B. With a prompt, you can have GitHub Copilot create data, such as for logins. This can also be in a certain format, such as JSON. As for the other answers, GitHub does not use

randomization to generate data. Also, the AI model does not create data that is streamed in real time or sensor data. For this, you need to use specialized tools.

6. D. Because of its training on an extensive dataset, GitHub Copilot can be useful for all phases of the SDLC process.

7. A. The GitHub Copilot REST API gives you access to usage metrics. Examples include the number of suggestions generated and the acceptance rates. This can help an organization measure the impact of the tool.

8. C. GitHub Copilot can convert code from one language to another. But this process is far from perfect. The code translation is really meant as an initial step, which should be followed up with more extensive analysis and review.

9. A. DevOps is an approach where development and operations teams work together. This helps with continuous integration, frequent updates, and automated testing.

10. B. With GitHub Copilot, you can refactor your code. This helps enhance readability, maintainability, and performance without changing the underlying functionality.

11. D. The context window limits the amount of code GitHub Copilot can process at a time. This means that it may not capture the full impact of the code refactoring.

12. C. GitHub Copilot is trained on extensive amounts of scripts for SQL. The result is that it can be a powerful tool when working with databases.

13. C. With GitHub Copilot, you can add one or more files for your requirements notes. Then you can write a prompt to create a requirements document.

14. C. The extract method is a type of refactoring. It involves breaking down a large function into smaller, more manageable ones. This is something that GitHub Copilot can perform.

15. A. This is the endpoint to use when accessing metrics about the use of GitHub in your enterprise.

16. C. You can use a prompt in GitHub Copilot. But a better approach is to use the GitHub Copilot for Azure extension, which is trained specifically for Azure deployment.

17. D. The `/explain` short-code will break down the complexities and attempt to understand what the code does.

18. C. You highlight the code and use `/explain`. GitHub Copilot will understand that you want to know how the regular expression works.

19. A. Because of the context window of the LLM, there is a fixed limit of how much information it can handle at once. This means it can miss important relationships.

20. D. This uses two short-code commands for your prompt: `/fix` and `/explain`. This will not only identify the logic error but will also provide an explanation.

Chapter 7: Testing and Privacy Considerations

1. B. The purpose of software testing is to ensure that the application does what it is intended to do. It is a core phase of the SDLC process.

2. B. The focus of unit testing it to test individual functions or blocks of software code. It helps spot errors earlier in the process.

3. D. Unit testing will test individual parts of a codebase, not how they interact with each other. For this, you need to use integration testing.

4. C. Unit testing should be focused on one function or task. This helps isolate the root cause of the problem.

5. A. With TDD, you will write the tests before implementing the code. This is to help ensure that the code meets requirements and is reliable from the start.

6. B. Keeping unit tests independent helps isolate failures. This makes it easier to identify and fix issues.

7. D. With integration testing, you test how the different components of the code interact. This can identify bugs and conflicts.

8. C. With top-down integration testing, the tests begin with the higher-level modules. You then add the lower-level modules incrementally.

9. B. GitHub Copilot automates the process of creating unit tests. It does this by generating boilerplate tests that are based on the relevant function or class.

10. A. By using /tests in a prompt, GitHub Copilot will create boilerplate unit tests.

11. B. With /tests, you cannot customize it, such as for the test framework. You need to write a custom prompt for this.

12. A. While GitHub Copilot can create useful unit tests, they are usually not complete. You can use coverage tools to help out. You should also do a code review.

13. A. A mock prevents an actual network request. Rather, it will simulate this process. This means that the result of the test will not be impacted by other factors, which could make it tough to determine the root cause of the issue.

14. B. Providing more details for the scenarios in the prompt can be helpful, such as with HTTP errors, invalid JSON responses, and timeouts.

15. D. Privacy is a major priority for GitHub. The company has a set of principles that include respecting user data, transparency, and privacy by design.

16. A. GitHub offers various ways to protect privacy, such as by making profiles private and hiding email addresses.

17. B. For organization-wide policy management and file exclusion, you need either the Business or Enterprise edition of GitHub Copilot.

18. D. Audit logs, exclusion of files, and blocking of suggestions matching public code are all only part of the Business and Enterprise editions of GitHub Copilot. This is generally because these tools are focused on larger organizations, which have more privacy needs.

19. B. Contention exclusions will protect sensitive data—like API keys, passwords and personal user information—from being indexed for code suggestions.

20. A. A reason GitHub may not generate suggestions is that the extension is outdated.

Index

Online Test Bank

To help you study for your GitHub Copilot certification exam, register to gain one year of FREE access after activation to the online interactive test bank—included with your purchase of this book!

To access our learning environment, simply visit www.wiley.com/go/ sybextestprep, follow the instructions to register your book, and instantly gain one year of FREE access after activation to:

- All of the chapter questions from this book, so you can practice in a timed and graded setting for the GitHub Copilot certification exam.
- A set of 100 flashcards
- A searchable glossary
- A 65-question practice exam

Printed and bound by CPI Group (UK) Ltd, Croydon, CR0 4YY

05/08/2025

14713995-0001